The Apostles' Creed:

Articles of Faith for the 21st Century

Resources for Catholic Administrators and Religious Educators in Knowledge of the Faith

Brian Schmisek, Ph.D.

National Catholic Educational Association

Cover photo inset: © 2008 iStockphoto.com / Sanna Wicks

St. Peter's Basilica, Vatican City. Statue in foreground is St. Peter, with statues of the
saints and Christ visible along the top of the edifice.

ISBN No. 1-55833-419-X

Part No. REL-24-1413

To my parents, John and Rita,
who sacrificed to send their children
to Catholic Schools

Contents

Editor's Preface

At the opening of the Second Vatican Council in 1962, Blessed John XXIII (1958-1963) said to the bishops gathered from around the world: "Christian doctrine should be guarded and taught more efficaciously." While it is the duty of every baptized Christian to pass on the faith, some are especially charged with teaching and catechizing roles. For those who say yes to God's call to teach the faith, the baptismal duty takes on a privileged character. Not only are they called to be authentic witnesses of the faith in word and deed, but they are also held to a higher standard of knowledge of the faith. In a post-Vatican II era of renewal, a steady stream of catechetical directories, documents and resources have emerged to guide those who participate in specific ways in the teaching mission of the Church. To facilitate an organic unity to handing on the faith, the *General Directory for Catechesis* (1997) identifies six universal tasks for catechesis that work together and build on one another: catechesis promotes knowledge of the faith, catechesis promotes knowledge of the meaning of the Liturgy and the Sacraments, catechesis teaches Christians how to pray with Christ, catechesis prepares Christians to live in community and to participate in the life and mission of the Church, and catechesis promotes a missionary spirit that prepares the faithful to be present as Christians in society.

The *National Directory for Catechesis* (2005) describes the first of these catechetical tasks "promoting knowledge of the faith" in these words:

The initial proclamation of the Gospel introduces the hearers to Christ for the first time and invites conversion to him. By the action of the Holy Spirit, such an encounter engenders in the hearers a desire to know about Christ, his life, and the content of his message. Catechesis responds to this desire by giving the believers a knowledge of the content of God's self-revelation, which is found in Sacred Scripture and Sacred Tradition, and by introducing them to the meaning of the Creed. Creeds and doctrinal formulas that state the Church's beliefs are expressions of the Church's living tradition, which from the time of the apostles has developed "in the Church with the help of the Holy Spirit." (DV, no. 8)

To advance this essential task of promoting knowledge of the faith, the Department of Religious Education presents this publication in the series titled, *For Religious Educators,* as a resource for teachers, catechists and interested readers.

I thank Dr. Brian Schmisek for writing *The Apostles' Creed: Articles of Faith for the Twenty-First Century.* Drawing from research for his doctoral dissertation from The Catholic University of America on the Apostles' Creed, he makes accessible the history and development of the early creedal statement of the Church in an interesting and lively manner. By including practical applications, summary statements and reflection questions for each article, he provides readers with a resource to use alone or in a small group to deepen ones knowledge of the faith.

I also thank and acknowledge Lisa Pannucci in the Department of Religious Education for assisting me in managing the project, Christina Gergits for editorial assistance, and Mary Twillman for her expertise with the cover, design and production of the text.

Diana Dudoit Raiche
Executive Director
Department of Religious Education

Foreword

As Catholics, we hold the Apostles' Creed as a great gift summarizing the belief of the early apostles and calling us to share in that same faith. Two thousand years later we still hold this Creed as an important summary of our faith and a link to the first apostles of the Church.

We are fortunate that Dr. Brian Schmisek has placed in writing a very helpful study of the Apostles' Creed and discusses it in a way that it continues to relate to the 21st century. I believe all those involved in religious education and evangelization will benefit from this reading. It is a real treasure.

The following pages explain the theology of the 12 articles of faith in the Apostles' Creed, their roots in apostolic faith and how they can be applied to our spiritual lives today in living out our Catholic faith. The writings also apply the great gift of the Apostles' Creed to today's parish religious educators and Catholic school teachers.

There is a great hunger in our Church today to know the teachings of the Church as rooted in Christ and the apostles. This book is very timely and will be helpful for all Catholics, especially for those who have taken on important roles of leadership in catechetical ministry. Through the reading of this insightful book people will be called to grow in faith and then to be able to invite others to grow in that faith, the faith of the apostles as it continues today.

Many Catholics today are eager to delve into the teachings of the Church and to learn more about them historically, theologically and spiritually. This book gives Catholics and others an opportunity to study more about our faith and its relevance today.

The Apostles' Creed is a great gift to our Church. We want this Creed to move us to live our lives as the disciples of the Lord Jesus in deeper faith and with greater conviction.

I am deeply grateful to NCEA and to Dr. Brian Schmisek for this helpful book which enables us to ponder more deeply the great gift of the Apostles' Creed.

Bishop Gregory M. Aymond
Diocese of Austin

Author's Preface

This book is written primarily for Catholic school teachers, parish catechetical leaders, and Catechists who desire a basic knowledge of Catholic faith as articulated in the Apostles' Creed. It is my hope that this book explains the meaning of the twelve articles of faith, their roots in apostolic faith, and their applicability and meaning for today's religious educator, and Catholic school teacher.

The introduction covers background issues pertaining to the Apostles' Creed. For example, it was not actually written by the apostles but is based on the "Old Roman Creed." The Apostles' Creed was influential in Reformation debates and formed the basis of a major section of the Roman Catechism following the Council of Trent. The Apostles' Creed even forms the basis of a section the *Catechism of the Catholic Church* today.

Following the introduction are twelve chapters, each covering an article of the creed. Each chapter begins with the article itself, how its roots are present in Sacred Scripture (in some cases both the Old Testament and the New Testament), what the article meant for early Christians, (i.e., what theological truth it was conveying), how the article may have been understood later, and how the article can be understood today, looking variously at the new catechism, the *US Catholic Catechism for Adults*, and some contemporary theologians. Each chapter concludes with a summary of the theological import of the article. Discussion questions are also posed for those who study this material in a group setting, but the questions may also be fruitful as individual reflection questions. The questions are designed not only to review some material, but also to apply it, by thinking about its relevance and meaning for today. Though not every chapter includes each element, this is the basic structure of the book. The final chapter of the book is a conclusion.

In a book on this subject matter, recourse to the sources is fundamental. Though knowledge of Hebrew, Greek, and Latin are not presumed, many pertinent sections are transliterated. At times the original text is given in the endnotes for those with facility in the language. Further discussion of certain material, or more extensive documentation of an argument can be found in the notes. Yet, the book is designed to be read without recourse to the notes for those who might find that burdensome. All non-scriptural translations are my own unless otherwise indicated.

This section would not be complete without gratitude expressed to Diana Dudoit Raiche who suggested this project to me. As fellow graduate students at The Catholic University of America, and now as colleagues in religious education, it would be an honor if some of her dynamic energy and vision for a more theologically informed laity were translated to these pages.

Finally, thanks to Marnie, John, Clare, Peter, and Helen. Their witness is simply powerful and understated.

Abbreviations of Sources

AB	Anchor Bible
ABD	Anchor Bible Dictionary
ABRL	Anchor Bible Reference Library
ACW	Ancient Christian Writers
AH	*Adversus Haereses*, Irenaeus
CCC	Catechism of the Catholic Church 2nd ed.
CCSL	Corpus Christianorum: Series latina
CSEL	Corpus scriptorum ecclesiasticorum latinorum
DS	H. Denzinger and A. Schönmetzer. *Enchiridion symbolorum definitionum et declarationum de rebus fidei et morum.* 35th Edition.
ECC	J.N.D. Kelly. *Early Christian Creeds.* 3rd ed. Singapore: Longman, 1972.
EEC	*Encyclopedia of the Early Church.* 2 vols. Oxford: New York, 1992.
LW	*Luther's Works.* 55 vols. American ed., 1959.
LXX	*Septuaginta*
NJBC	R. E. Brown, J. A. Fitzmyer, and R. E. Murphy. *The New Jerome Biblical Commentary.*
NRSV	New Revised Standard Version
PG	J. Migne (ed.) *Patrologia graeca*
PL	J. Migne (ed.) *Patrologia latina*
SacPag	Sacra Pagina
SC	Sources chrétiennes
TAG	J. A. Fitzmyer. *To Advance the Gospel: New Testament Studies.* 2nd ed.
TDNT	G. Kittel and G. Friedrich. *Theological Dictionary of the New Testament.*
Q'	Theodotion version
USCCA	*United States Catholic Catechism for Adults.* 2006

Miscellaneous Abbreviations

bis   twice

ca.   *circa* (about)

cf.   confer (compare, consult)

d.   died

e.g.   *exampla gratia* (for [the sake of an] example)

et al.   *et alia* (and others)

fl.   *floruit* (flourished)

i.e.   *id est* (that is)

r.   reigned

ter   thrice

The Apostles' Creed: Articles of Faith for the 21st Century

Introduction

The Apostles' Creed, with its twelve articles of faith, is familiar to many Catholics who pray the Rosary. Catholics also hear and/or recite the Apostles' Creed at liturgies with children. The Creed we say at a regular Sunday liturgy is usually referred to as the Nicene Creed. These two creeds, the Apostles' Creed and the Nicene Creed, hold a special place in the life of the church (CCC §193). Yet, neither encompasses the entirety of the Catholic faith.

It is commonly assumed that the Apostles' Creed is so named because it comes from the Twelve Apostles. Legend has it that each apostle contributed one article.[1] However, we know today that the Apostles' Creed has a history much more complex. Instead of indicating that the creed comes directly from the twelve apostles, the term "apostles' creed" is used to mean that the creed reflects what the apostles believed and taught.

The term creed comes from the Latin "*credo*" which means "I believe." (The Greek term is *symbolon*, [in English, *symbol*] which the Catechism uses with some frequency). A creed is then a statement of faith. In some ways we can say Christians have had creeds from the earliest days. Indeed, St. Paul seems to appeal to a creed when he says, "Jesus is Lord" (Rom 10:9). Philip baptizes the Ethiopian eunuch after he proclaims, "I believe that Jesus Christ is the Son of God" (Acts 8:37). We know that these early creeds grew in content so that it was no longer enough to claim Jesus is Lord. Paul says in his letter to the Corinthians, "yet for us there is one God, the Father, from whom all things are and for whom we exist, and one Lord, Jesus Christ, through whom all things are and through whom we exist." (1 Cor 8:6). There also is the famous example of 1 Tim 2:3-6 which seems to draw on a creedal statement to explicate the "knowledge of the truth:"

> *This is good and pleasing to God our savior, who wills everyone to be saved and to come to knowledge of the truth. For there is one God. There is also one mediator between God and the human race, Christ Jesus, himself human, who gave himself as ransom for all. This was the testimony at the proper time.*

Early versions of creeds also grew to express other key aspects of faith in Jesus. For example, Ignatius of Antioch, who wrote seven letters on his way to martyrdom in Rome (d. ca. 117) wrote:

> *Stop your ears, therefore, when any one speaks to you at variance with Jesus Christ, who was descended from David, and was also of Mary; who was truly born, and did eat and drink. He was truly persecuted under Pontius Pilate; He was truly crucified, and [truly] died, in the sight of beings in heaven, and on earth, and under the earth. He was also truly raised from the dead, His Father quickening Him, even as after the same manner His Father will so raise up us who believe in Him by Christ Jesus, apart from whom we do not possess the true life.[2]*

Furthermore, there was a desire not only to express faith in Jesus and the key aspects of his life and death, but there was also a need to profess a belief in God the Father, and in the Spirit. For example, at the close of the Gospel of Matthew, Jesus gives his disciples a command:

> *Go, therefore, and make disciples of all nations, baptizing them in the name of the Father, and of the Son, and of the holy Spirit, teaching them to observe all that I have commanded you. And behold, I am with you always, until the end of the age." (Matt 28:19-20).*

This command to baptize in the name of the Father and of the Son and of the Holy Spirit may have given rise to the practice of professing faith in the context of baptism. For, ultimately a creed was professed by the catechumens immediately prior to baptism. Sometimes the catechumen was questioned (as we do today at times in the liturgy) and in so doing made a profession of faith in God the Father, Jesus the Son, and the Holy Spirit. With each name, the catechumen was plunged into the waters of baptism so that profession in the triune God was accompanied by a triune plunge! In fact, Hippolytus, writing about A.D. 215 tells us how baptisms were being done, and thus gives us an early form of the creed. Note the Christological section will share some affinities with the quasi-creedal formula of Ignatius of Antioch cited above.

> *When the elder takes hold of each of them who are to receive baptism, he shall tell each of them to renounce, saying, "I renounce you Satan, all your service, and all your works." After he has said this, he shall anoint each with the Oil of Exorcism, saying, "Let every evil spirit depart from you." Then, after these things, the bishop passes each of them on nude to the elder who stands at the water. They shall stand in the water naked. A deacon, likewise, will go down with them into the water. When each of them to be baptized has gone down into the water, the one baptizing shall lay hands on each of them, asking, "Do you believe in God the Father Almighty?" And the one being baptized shall answer, "I believe." He shall then baptize each of them once, laying his hand upon each of their heads. Then he shall ask, "Do you believe in Jesus Christ, the Son of God, who was born of the Holy Spirit and the Virgin Mary, who was crucified under Pontius Pilate, and died, and rose on the third day living from the dead, and ascended into heaven, and sat down at the right hand of the Father, the one coming to judge the living and the dead?" When each has answered, "I believe," he shall baptize a second time. Then he shall ask, "Do you believe in the Holy Spirit and the Holy Church and the resurrection of the flesh?" Then each being baptized shall answer, "I believe." And thus let him baptizo the third time.[3]*

As we can imagine, there were no sacramentaries in the early church. As a friend of mine likes to say, "Jesus did not hand out three-ring binders at the last supper." Different locales practiced the faith in a variety of ways, especially in the first centuries of the church. We should not be too surprised to find that while many ancient creeds were similar, it is not possible to say that all creeds were the same. Rather than one distinct formula memorized by all churches everywhere throughout the Ancient Christian Mediterranean, there were a variety of creedal statements, and most likely a variety of creeds even in the same city, perhaps even in various liturgical settings. Moreover, the creed itself, along with the Lord's Prayer, sacraments, and other cultic rituals were not to be written down on paper, but on the heart.

It seems that a basic three article formula (not unlike Matthew 28:19-20) was expanded in different ways, at different times, by a variety of communities, to express the faith of the believing community. These creedal statements were seen as legitimate expressions of faith even though they may have differed on certain details (cf. CCC §192-193).

A variety of ancient authors give witness to the creeds that were spoken: Rufinus, Jerome, Tertullian, Justin, Irenaeus, Hippolytus, and others. These authorities might mention a particular creed and reference its locale. For example, we hear that there was a creed in Aquileia (ancient city in Italy near modern day Venice) and a creed in Rome. The latter is known today as the "Old Roman Creed." The Apostles' Creed seems to have been a variant of this "Old Roman Creed."

Old Roman Creed

The Old Roman Creed is a name used by scholars to refer to a creed used in Rome that is attested by many sources. We do not have any ancient source saying, "this is the Old Roman Creed" and then proceeding to deliver it. Instead, we have ancient sources saying that this is the creed in Rome. Some authorities give us a Latin version. Others give us a Greek version. Scholars deduce that the Greek version is more primitive, thus pointing to its being the "original" language of the Old Roman Creed. Others suggest the Greek version was used for Greek-speaking catechumens and the Latin version was used for the Latin-speaking catechumens.

A creed in Greek is not so far-fetched as Paul wrote his letter to the Romans in Greek, and the Gospel of Mark, often associated with the church at Rome, was written in Greek. For that matter, the entire New Testament was written in Greek. Since the Roman church still spoke Greek in the 2nd century, that seems a likely date for the origin of the Old Roman Creed.

There are many witnesses to a creed in Rome. For example, the *Apostolic Traditions* cited above, is associated with the Roman church. Tertullian (b. ca. A.D. 160) also tells us about a creed at Rome. He was born a pagan in Carthage, became a Christian by 197, and was ordained a priest about 200. Sometime after 206 he seems to have become a Montanist (follower of Montanus, a mid-second century heretic). By 213 Tertullian had completely separated from the church. He even separated from the Montanists and formed his own sect which became known as the Tertullianists. Augustine himself later reconciled the Tertullianists with the church.

Writing as a Christian, Tertullian reflects the teaching of the church at Rome: "[The church at Rome] acknowledges one God and Lord, the creator of the universe, and Christ Jesus (born) of the virgin Mary, son of God the creator, and the resurrection of the flesh; the law and the prophets [the church at Rome] unites with the gospels and the apostolic writings…"[4] While a Montanist, Tertullian wrote another work in which he makes attestation to a creed:

> *The rule of faith is altogether one, alone unchangeable and irreformable: namely, of believing in one God almighty, creator of the world, and his son Jesus Christ, born of the virgin Mary, crucified under Pontius Pilate, raised on the third day from the dead, received into heaven, now seated at the right hand of the Father, to come again to judge the living and the dead also through the resurrection of the flesh.*[5]

Other theologians bearing witness to the Old Roman Creed include Rufinus, a contemporary of Jerome, who compares it with his own creed of Aquileia. The Old Roman Creed is also attested in Greek by Marcellus, bishop of

Ancyra in Cappodocia, in an Apologia to Pope Julius I dated to 340, and preserved in Epiphanius, *Panarion*. 72.3.1. Rufinus compares the creed of his baptism at Aquilea with the creed professed at Rome. He admits that the Aquilean creed has some additions, while maintaining that the creed has apostolic origin.

So, the Old Roman Creed is attested but must be reconstructed based on scholarship, with the knowledge that other scholars may propose other, more convincing reconstructions. For example, we may compare the creed at Rome given to us by Rufinus (in Latin), with the creed at Rome given to us by Marcellus (in Greek). There are slight differences between the two, but differences nonetheless even besides the issue of language.

Reproduced here is the creed of Rome attested by Rufinus, reconstructed by J.N.D. Kelly. Note the differences between this creed and the Apostles' Creed we recite today.

I believe in God the Father almighty
      And in Christ Jesus, His only Son, our Lord,
            Who was born from the Holy Spirit and the Virgin Mary,
            Who was crucified under Pontius Pilate and buried,
on the third day He rose again from the dead,
            He ascended to heaven,
            He sits at the Father's right hand,
            Whence He will come to judge the living and the dead;
      And in the Holy Spirit,
            the holy Church,
            the remission of sins,
            the resurrection of the flesh.[6]

Apostles' Creed

The Apostles' Creed[7] is first referred to as such in a letter from Ambrose in 389. After calling it the "Apostles' creed," Ambrose says that "the spotless Roman church has always guarded and saved [it]."[8] As cited above, Rufinus was convinced of the apostolic origin of the creed and even mentioned how at Pentecost each apostle made a contribution to it before setting out to preach. Augustine commented on the creed in Sermon 398, also known as,

On the Creed to the Catechumens. Later in *De symbolo* Augustine (rather a late pseudo-Augustine)[9] claimed that each apostle contributed one article:

> *How each apostle composed the creed..... On the tenth day after the ascension, when the disciples had gathered in fear of the Jews, the Lord sent the Spirit as he promised. It came as a glittering sword aflame. And filled with the knowledge of all languages they composed the creed.*
>
> *Peter said, "I believe in God the Father almighty." ...*
>
> *Andrew said, "and in Jesus Christ his Son."...*
>
> *James said, "Who was conceived by the Holy Spirit... Born of the Virgin Mary."...John said, "suffered under Pontius Pilate ...was crucified, died, and was buried,*
>
> *according to the flesh."...*
>
> *Thomas said, "He descended into hell...on the third day he rose from the dead."...*
>
> *James said, "He ascended into heaven ...he is seated at the right hand of God, the*
>
> *Father almighty."...*
>
> *Philip said, "from there he will come to judge the living and the dead."...*
>
> *Bartholomew said, "I believe in the Holy Spirit"...*
>
> *Matthew said, "The Holy Catholic Church...the communion of saints"...*
>
> *Simon said, "the remission of sins"...*
>
> *Thaddaeus said, "the resurrection of the flesh"...*
>
> *Matthias said, "Life eternal."...[10]*

Interestingly, the list of the twelve used for the creed comes from the gospel of Matthew ("the church's gospel") with the name of Matthias in place of Judas, as told in Acts 1:26. Yet, the list of the twelve from Acts names Jude of James as one of the twelve instead of Thaddaeus (see "Lists of the Twelve" in the appendices). The New Testament itself does not agree on the list of the twelve apostles. We are forced to follow either the Markan/Matthean tradition, or the Lucan tradition. The Gospel of John, with its fierce and overriding emphasis on Jesus, does not even bother to give us the list of the twelve.

Thus, the stage was set for the medieval period in the west. This "apostolic" catechetical instruction was a convenient tool for teaching the faith. Not until an attempt at reconciliation with the east at the Council of Florence in the 15th century was the credibility of the story credibility questioned. The east balked at the authority of the creed as they had never heard of it. Moreover, the creed was not in Sacred Scripture, nor in any of the early church fathers. With the advent of the renaissance, most serious scholars abandoned the idea that the creed had its verbatim origin with the apostles. Instead, they recognized that the creeds grew with the early church.

Luther arrived on the scene in the early 16th century. He is important for creedal studies because he changed one word of the Apostles' Creed: Catholic to Christian.[11] The Roman Catholic Church responded (in a way) by making the Apostles' Creed one of the bedrocks of the Roman Catechism that was produced in the wake of the Council of Trent. The Roman Catechism encapsulated the faith of the church for bishops and pastors around the four legs of Creed, Ten Commandments, Lord's Prayer, and Sacraments. The *Catechism of the Catholic Church* published in the waning years of the 20th century followed the Roman Catechism's outline.

In the *Catechism of the Catholic Church* (between articles 184 and 185) we read the Apostles' Creed and the Nicene Creed (see appendices at the back of this book). Moreover, the *Catechism* deals with creeds in general in §185-197.

This is the Apostles' Creed we recite today:

I BELIEVE IN GOD, the Father almighty, creator of heaven and earth.

and in Jesus Christ, his only Son, our Lord,

> who was conceived by the power of the Holy Spirit

> born of the Virgin Mary,

> suffered under Pontius Pilate,

> was crucified, died, and was buried.

> He descended into hell.

> On the third day he rose again from the dead.

> He ascended into heaven

> and is seated at the right hand of God the Father Almighty.

> From thence he shall come again to judge the living and the dead.

I believe in the Holy Spirit,

the holy catholic Church,

the communion of saints,

the forgiveness of sins,

the resurrection of the body,

and the life everlasting.

Amen.

Article

I

I believe in
God the Father
almighty creator
of heaven and
earth.

Article 1.   I believe in God the Father almighty creator of heaven and earth.

The English translation "I believe" reflects the Latin "credo." Each Christian professes a personal faith in common with the community of believers so that the faith I profess is the faith "we profess."

In some ways it is surprising that the Apostles' Creed, with its twelve articles of faith, has only one article addressing "God the Father." We can surmise immediately that this article is not one over which Christians are arguing, or debating. It needs little clarification (unlike the profession of faith in Jesus Christ his Son, deserving of six articles, or half of the creed).

Old Testament

The appellations of God from this article all stem from the Old Testament where God is called Father (Ps 68:5; 89:26; Isa 9:6), almighty (Gen 17:1; 28:3; 35:11; 43:14; 48:3; Exod 6:3; Ps 68:14; 91:1; Ez 10:5; Joel 1:15; Wis 7:25; Sir 42:17; 50:14); and creator of heaven and earth (Gen 1:1; 2:4; Isa 40:28; Neh 9:6; Ps 33:6-9).

Father

The term Father in the Old Testament was applied to God in the sense that God was the father of Israel. Anthropomorphic images of God teaching Ephraim to walk convey the sense of God as parent (Hos 11:3). In Deut 1:31, God is portrayed as carrying the Israelites through the desert as a man carries his child. The sense of God as parent is also evident in the metaphor of God hovering over his brood as an eagle would (Deut 32:10-12). God was also father to the king (2 Sam 7:14). This image of God as Father was certainly apparent in the ministry of Jesus (e.g., John 6:27), who taught his disciples to address God as Pater (in Greek), Abba (in Aramaic), or Father. St. Paul gives evidence that the second generation Christians indeed cried "Abba" (Rom 8:15; Gal 6:4). The father image is thus meant to convey authority as well as loving care, concern, and protection.

Thus, for the early Christians, calling God Father echoed the faith expressed in the Old Testament. The God of the Old Testament was the God of Jesus Christ, the God of the New Testament, the God of the Christians. A challenge to this line of thinking was made by the second century heretic Marcion. He believed that the Old Testament God was so unlike the God of Jesus Christ that the Old Testament itself was inspired by the devil. Early Christians fought Marcionite thought by maintaining that both the Old Testament and the New Testament were inspired by the same God, the one God and Father of Jesus Christ.

Despite the fact that Jesus himself, the early Christians, and centuries of Christians from then on addressed God as Father, some today find that term, or any other masculine referent for God, inadequate. Some modern theologians query whether "father language" is entirely apropos when speaking of God, for God is ultimately neither male nor female.[12] These theologians claim that the father language arose in a patriarchal world that no longer corresponds to our own. Moreover, mothers are able to express loving care, concern, and protection as fathers do. It is important to note that the Catechism of the Catholic Church says, "God's paternal tenderness can also be expressed by the image of motherhood."[13] The catechism cites two scripture passages: Isa 66:13 and Ps 131:2. While some modern theologians are raising our awareness of the issues surrounding paternal images of God, the image of God as father is dominant in the scriptural, liturgical, and theological tradition.

Almighty

"Almighty" is a title for God associated with the patriarchs (Abraham, Isaac, and Joseph) (e.g., Gen 17:1; 28:3; 35:11; 43:14; 48:3; Exod 6:3). The Hebrew term underlying "God Almighty" is "*El-Shaddai*." There were many various titles for God such as God of the Mountain (*El-Har*), God Most High (*El-Elyon*, Gen 14:18), God of Vision (*El-Roi*; Gen 16:13), God Everlasting (*El-Olam*; Gen 21:33), God of Bethel (or, *El-Bethel*, or God of the house of god; Gen 31:13; 35:1,3,7), God the God of Israel (*El-Elohe-Israel*; Gen 33:20), God the God of your fathers (*El-Elohe-Abikah*; Gen 46:3), Shield (*Magen*; Gen 15:1), and many others. Yet, in the midst of all these names for God, the term *El-Shaddai*, or God Almighty stands out because of its association with the patriarchs. It is an ancient title for God. In the story of God's self-revelation to Moses, God says, "I am the LORD [*YHWH*]. As God the Almighty [*El-Shaddai*] I appeared to Abraham, Isaac and Jacob, but my name, LORD, [*YHWH*] I did not make known to them." (Exod 6:2-3).

In the Exodus passage we see that *El-Shaddai* and YHWH are one and the same. They are not two gods. The same God whom the patriarchs worshipped as *El-Shaddai* now calls Moses. But now, God reveals his name as YHWH. This name is also known as the "tetragrammaton" or "four-letters." This name was holy and not to be pronounced. In Greek manuscripts of the Old Testament, the four letters were often rendered as *kyrios*, or "Lord," if they were rendered at all. In the New American Bible, this highly respected name for God is rendered by the all capitals, LORD. So, any time we read "LORD" in the New American Bible we recognize that the underlying Hebrew is *YHWH*.

The root meaning of *shaddai* is disputed. Scholars differ on its etymology. Those who translated the term into Greek or Hebrew often used "*pantokrator*," and "*omnipotens*," thus indicating that the term meant for them "powerful one, strong one, or almighty." That same Greek term *pantokrator* was used of God in the New Testament. Interestingly, in 2 Cor 6:18 Paul calls God pantokrator immediately after referring to God as father (Paul is freely quoting 2 Sam 7:14). *Pantokrator* is also a frequent term in Revelation. When St. Jerome translated the Hebrew Old Testament into

Latin, he often used the term *Deus omnipotens*, or God All-powerful/Almighty for *El-Shaddai*. These Greek and Latin terms then are a clue for us that in the creed, the underlying term for *omnipotens*, or *pantocrator*, is ultimately the Hebrew term *shaddai*. The God of the Old Testament, the God of the fathers Abraham, Isaac, and Jacob, is the same God of the Christians.

Creator

Another Old Testament appellation of God repeated in the Creed is "Creator of heaven and earth." This is significant in that many myths of the ancient near east posited that the earth had been made of the dead bodies of gods, or the sun, moon, and stars were themselves gods. Genesis 1 relates that God created the earth, the seas, the heavens, and all they contain. The sun is not a god but is a "big light" placed in the sky by God to govern the day. The moon is not a god but is a "little light" placed in the sky by God to govern the night. The sky itself is a firmament established by God by the voice of his command. Creation was not difficult work for God; it was not labor intensive. Moreover creation itself is not God. God is distinct from creation.

God is also a good creator. Seven times the narrator of the first creation story tells the reader that God saw that it was good. After the sixth day creation is declared "very good." This is an important lesson for us in the modern world. The created world is good, and it is a source of goodness. Creation itself may be seen as God's first revelation. We human beings learn something of the creator by studying creation. Rather than a source of evil and temptation, creation is something good, even very good. More than that, creation is ultimately a free gift. These ideas forming the opening of the Bible may be read throughout the sacred canon, and into the New Testament (Rom 1:25; 1 Pet 4:19). It comes as no surprise then to read this basic affirmation of faith in the first article of the Apostles' Creed.

New Testament

Ultimately, the earliest followers of Jesus (who were Jews) knew that they were worshipping the same God that they had always worshipped, the same God that Jesus himself had worshipped. The God of the Old Testament and the God of the New Testament are the same. Marcion's ideas were thus condemned as heretical.

It might be fascinating to ask ourselves what we really believe about God the Father. Most often what we say about God the Father in ordinary, everyday speech is what we mean when we talk about "God" in general. The *Catechism* tells us that the Father language is used to express authority and loving care (§ 239).

Summary

There is a God. God reveals himself as a Father to his chosen people, to Jesus his son, to all. Father image expresses the love, and the power (authority) of God. By his love, God calls a people and makes them his own. By his power, he creates the heavens and the earth. As creator, God is distinct from creation. God is not creation but is its source. Thus, Christians respect and care for creation, but do not worship it.

DISCUSSION QUESTIONS
cf. CCC §198-421

1. What in particular makes the first person of the Trinity unique?
2. At what times in your own prayer life do you address God as "Father"? What other names do you use to address God?
3. How does your relationship with your own father inform or distract from calling God "Father"?
4. How would you demonstrate that the God of the Old Testament is the same God of the New Testament?

Article

II

I believe in Jesus
Christ, his only
Son, our Lord.

Article 2. I believe in Jesus Christ, his only Son, our Lord.

The second article begins with the Latin verb *credo*, or "I believe," signaling that this is now a new topic, as it were. We are no longer talking about God the Father, but now we are proclaiming belief in "Jesus," the second person of the Trinity. We will see that most of the articles in the creed have to do with Jesus, because the issues at stake during the formulation of the creed were primarily Christological. That is, the theological debates centered on the person of Jesus, his identity, and what God has done through him for humanity. So, we are not surprised to find half of the articles in the creed about Jesus, and only one about God the Father.

Jesus

The name Jesus sets the second person in the Trinity in a historical context. The Greek name *Iēsous* is derived from the Hebrew name *Yēshû*, a shortened form of the Hebrew name *Yeshûa* (Ezra 2:2; Neh 3:19) which itself is a contraction of *Yĕhôshuā* (Josh 1:1) "Yahweh, help!" These Hebrew names were common.[14] In some ways we can say it is equivalent to the name "Josh" as a shortened form of Joshua.[15] This name was common in the first century, almost like "Bob," or "John" today.

The creed, like many New Testament authors, uses Christ

of Jesus almost as a last name. Indeed, one grade schooler told me that Jesus Christ was the son of Mary and Joseph Christ. But of course, "Christ" is not the last name of Jesus. It is instead a title, based on the Greek term *Christos* which is itself a translation of the Hebrew term *mashîā,* or Messiah, used in the Old Testament to refer to historical kings of Israel (e.g., 1 Sam 16:6), often of David (e.g., 2 Sam 1:14), and even the pagan king Cyrus (Isa 45:1). At times it is used as an adjective for a high priest (e.g., Lev 4:5). [16] So today, when we call Jesus the Christ, we are saying that he is the Messiah.

Christ

Messiah, or Christ, is one of the earliest titles for Jesus. For example, Paul interpreted God's revelation of his Son to/in him (Gal 1:16) in messianic terms. Jesus was the Messiah (Rom 9:5). By the time Paul wrote his letters, he used "Christ" as something of a second name for Jesus.

However, it is important to recall that Jesus did not fulfill the role of Messiah the way first century Jews thought it would be fulfilled. That is, many first century Jews expected a Davidic King who would restore the independence of Israel, casting off Roman occupation, and thereby bringing peace and prosperity to the people. Certainly today, Jews do not believe Jesus is, or was, the Messiah (though "Messianic Jews" exist, they are not considered Jews by most Jews [as they profess belief in Christ], or Christians by most Christians [for they do not accept the divinity of Christ]).

Once at an interreligious dialogue at the University of Dallas, a freshman asked the rabbi a question that perhaps only a freshman can ask, "Why don't you Jews just accept the fact that Jesus is the Messiah?" I say only a freshman can ask, because so many people have the question and are afraid to ask it. However, the rabbi did not shy away. He welcomed the question and then proceeded with this answer. Jews do not accept Jesus as the Messiah because he does not fulfill the job description. The Old Testament says nothing about a suffering Messiah. The Messiah is a Davidic King who will reign in Israel, establishing peace and prosperity. Jesus did not do that, so, for Jews, he is not the Messiah.

While the rabbi's response is correct from a strictly Jewish perspective, it is important to recognize that Christians believe Jesus fulfills what it means to be Messiah in a way that was completely unforeseen. Indeed the church states as much clearly when it says in the 2002 Pontifical Biblical Commission document, *The Jewish People and their Sacred Scripture in the Christian Bible*:

Christian faith recognises the fulfilment, in Christ, of the Scriptures and the hopes of Israel, but it does not understand this fulfilment as a literal one. Such a conception would be reductionist. In reality, in the mystery of Christ crucified and risen, fulfilment is brought about in a manner unforeseen. It includes transcendence. Jesus is not confined to playing an already fixed role — that of Messiah — but he confers, on the notions of Messiah and salvation, a fullness which could not have been imagined in advance; he fills them with a new reality; one can even speak in this connection of a "new creation". It would be wrong to consider the prophecies of the Old Testament as some kind of photographic anticipations of future events. All the texts, including those which later were read as messianic prophecies, already had an immediate import and meaning for their contemporaries before attaining a fuller meaning for future hearers. The messiahship of Jesus has a meaning that is new and original.[17]

So, only in faith can we say that Jesus is the Messiah, that Jesus is the Christ. He is King in the sense that he is establishing the Kingdom of God, with radically different values than the kingdom of this world.

Son of God

This article of the creed also mentions that Jesus is the only son of God. In this, the creed is echoing language from the gospel of John wherein the prologue states "only begotten of God." While it is true that Paul (Rom 8:15; Gal 4:6) and others claim that Jesus gives us the power to call God Father, Jesus is God's son in a unique way. We recall that at Jesus' baptism he is called God's son (Mark 1:11). Mark also tells us that Jesus cried "Abba" (the term for Father) in the garden of Gethsemane (Mark 14:36). Jesus, as unique son of God (John 1:16) gives others the power to call God Father. The most famous example would be the "Lord's Prayer," or the "Our Father" (Matt 6:9-13). When Jesus called God Father and said the Father and I are one, his enemies understood that as blasphemy, for he was making himself equal with God (John 5:18).

Lord

Finally, this article concludes, "our Lord." With this appellation, we come to what scholastic theologians termed, *Christus pro nobis*, or Christ for us. After we make the claims about who Jesus is, what does it mean to us? What is the salvific import of these Christological claims? For the Christian, Jesus is "our Lord."

In our English versions of the Old Testament we often come across the all capital letters, LORD as a way to refer to God. This all capital letter device is used to express the unpronounceable, untranslatable tetragrammaton, the four lettered name for God in the Hebrew Old Testament, YHWH. (Biblical Hebrew script uses only consonants. Vowels were inserted centuries later.) This four-lettered name of God was revealed to Moses.

> God also said to Moses, "I am the LORD. As God the Almighty I appeared to Abraham, Isaac and Jacob, but my name, LORD, I did not make known to them. (Exod 6:2-3).

In truth, the term YHWH does not mean "lord" but was rendered as such to avoid saying Yahweh. When a Jew came across this name in the sacred text, he would not pronounce it. Instead he would say "*adonaï*" which means, "lord." For example, in the Septuagint (the Greek translation of the Old Testament) the term YHWH is often rendered as *kyrios*, "lord." The Greek term kyrios also translates the Hebrew term *adôn* (LXX Ps 113:7) and the Aramaic *mare* (Dan Q' 2:47; 4:16,21; 5:23) each used in the Old Testament as a way to refer to God. [18]

The Greek term *kyrios* has a wide range of meanings. It can mean anything from "sir" (e.g. Matt 21:30) to "YHWH" (as we have seen). In this it might be better to think of the

Spanish term, señor. We may use this term to summon the waiter to bring more chips and salsa, but we can also use this term in the liturgy to speak of God. In English, the term "Lord" has more limited meaning. We would hardly speak of someone in daily life as "lord" but we do retain the term to speak of God. (As an aside, we do retain the term in the title, Monsignor, which literally means, "my Lord".)

As mentioned above, to indicate that the underlying Hebrew term is really YHWH, many English translations of the Bible will use the word Lord in all caps: LORD. There is still a hesitancy to translate YHWH as Yahweh in the Bible (despite all the songs we sing in church that seem to have no hesitation in using the term!).

So, when the early Christians began to call Jesus, *kyrios*, or Lord, they are expressing something significant, exalting Jesus to the status of YHWH. At times, the term really means nothing more than "sir" (e.g., John 4:11). But at other times it is clear that a titular meaning is intended. We know that early Christians were proclaiming the exalted status of the risen Christ as on par with YHWH. Perhaps nowhere is that more evident than in the hymn that Paul quotes to the Philippians which concludes: "every knee must bend and every tongue proclaim to the glory of God the father that Jesus Christ is Lord!" Though Paul himself sometimes uses *kyrios* for Yahweh (e.g., 1 Thess 4:6), he also applies the same title to Jesus. In the Philippians hymn, it suggests that Jesus is on par with Yahweh, though not to be identified with him (cf. Phil 2:11).

Even pagan sources tell us that the early Christians sang hymns to Christ as though he were God. For example, Pliny (ca. 63-113), the governor of Asia, had arrested some Christians. After he had them tortured they confessed that among other things, "on a set day they used to meet before dawn and sing a hymn among themselves to Christ, as though he were a god."[19]

The term "Lord" is also significant in the gospel of John. For example, John opens his gospel with the famous prologue, "In the beginning was the Word, and the Word was with God, and the Word was God" (John 1:1). The prologue continues to include the statement on incarnation, "And the word became made flesh and made his dwelling among us" (John 1:14a). Thus, from a narrative critical point of view, the implied reader knows this information about Jesus. Jesus is the Word of God made flesh, who lived among us. Not until the conclusion of the gospel,[20] after the death and resurrection of Jesus, does a human being (Thomas) proclaim, "My Lord and my God!" to which Jesus responds, "'Have you come to believe because you have seen me? Blessed are those who have not seen and have believed.' Now Jesus did many other signs in the presence of (his) disciples that are not written in this book. But these are written so that you may (come to) believe that Jesus is the Messiah, the Son of God, and that through this believe you may have life in his name" (John 20:28-30).

Thus, the term "Lord" in the Old Testament and in the New Testament has profound meaning. It was used in the Old Testament to refer to YHWH, and in the New Testament to express Jesus' identity for Christians. Jesus is on par with YHWH such that true faith in him leads to an expression of him as "my Lord and my God." This article in the creed echoes that early belief, Jesus Christ is our Lord.

Summary

Jesus was a historical figure who lived in Galilee in the early first century A.D. He was hailed as Christ, which means Messiah, or "anointed one" to designate that he was God's anointed. His relationship with God is so unique that he can be called God's only son (John 1:18). With respect to humanity, he is our Lord, on par with YHWH.

DISCUSSION QUESTIONS
cf. CCC §422-455

1. What do the titles, Messiah, and Lord, mean in their historical context? What do they mean to you? Is there a title you prefer to use for Jesus instead of Messiah or Lord? Why?
2. What does it mean that Jesus is the son of God?
3. What does it mean for us to be children of God?
4. How would you explain to a non-Christian what we believe by saying Jesus is the Christ?

Article

III

He was
conceived by
the power of
the Holy Spirit
and born of the
Virgin Mary.

*Article 3.   He was conceived by the power of the Holy
Spirit and born of the Virgin Mary.*

The third article reflects many of the
Christological debates that culminated in the
language "true God and true man." To say
that Jesus was conceived by the power of the
Holy Spirit echoes language of the gospels of
Matthew and Luke, the only New Testament accounts of the
birth of Jesus.

Born of the Virgin Mary

Though there is New Testament evidence that Mary is
the mother of Jesus (Matt 1:16; Mark 6:3; Luke 1:27-38; Acts
1:14),[21] neither Mark nor John mentions the virginal birth.
(The Gospel of John with its fierce overriding emphasis on
Jesus does not even give us Mary's name.) Matthew and
Luke are left to tell the story of the virgin birth.

At the conclusion of the genealogy of the Messiah,
Matthew says that "Jacob the father of Joseph, the husband
of Mary. Of her was born Jesus who is called the Messiah."
(Matt 1:16). He thus makes clear that Jesus was born of
Mary. At the same time, he also states clearly that Jesus
was conceived by the Holy Spirit so that he will be called
"Emmanuel" which means "God is with us" (Matt 1:20-25).
Matthew sees in the virgin birth a fulfillment of the prophecy in
Isaiah for he (Matthew) says,

behold, the angel of the Lord appeared to him in a dream and said, "Joseph, son of David, do not be afraid to take Mary your wife into your home. For it is through the Holy Spirit that this child has been conceived in her. She will bear a son and you are to name him Jesus, because he will save his people from their sins."

All this took place to fulfill what the Lord had said through the prophet: "Behold, the virgin shall be with child and bear a son, and they shall name him Emmanuel," which means "God is with us." (Matt 1:20-23).

It should be noted that in Isaiah the Hebrew text actually says, "Therefore the Lord himself will give you a sign. Look, the young woman is with child and shall bear a son, and shall name him Immanuel" (Isa 7:14 NRSV). Notice that the key term in Matthew "virgin" is "young woman" in the Isaiah text. Is Matthew playing fast and loose with scripture? The Hebrew term *almah* means "young woman," without respect to her virginity. When the Hebrew was translated into Greek in about the second century B.C., the Greek translators used the term *parthenos* to translate the Hebrew *almah*. The Greek term *parthenos* does mean "unmarried girl," or "virgin." Matthew, writing in Greek, was using the Greek version of what we call the Old Testament. So, he recognized that a virgin birth was the fulfillment of Scripture.

This is significant because Matthew is telling us that God was behind the miraculous birth of Jesus. Moreover, the virgin birth fulfills scripture. Matthew goes further in that when he lists the generations from Abraham he includes four women who also gave birth under difficult or abnormal circumstances: Tamar (1:3) Rahab (1:5a) Ruth (1:5b) and the wife of Uriah (1:6).

The story of Tamar is told in Genesis 38. She played the harlot and conceived the twins Perez and Zerah by her father-in-law Judah. Rahab (Joshua 2:6) was a harlot too. Living in Jericho, she helped the spies of Joshua and was therefore spared when that city was destroyed. Ruth was a Moabite who married into the people of Israel (Book of Ruth). The wife of Uriah's actual name of course is Bathsheeba. Matthew seems to employ verbal gymnastics to avoid even saying her name. David seduced Bathsheeba and had Uriah killed in battle (2 Sam 11-12). She later became the mother of Solomon. Why does Matthew mention these four women? Perhaps he is reminding us that the Davidic line has been peppered with unusual circumstances. Abnormalities are not abnormal with God. A virgin birth in fact fulfills scripture.

In Luke, the angel Gabriel announces to the Virgin Mary that she is to bear a son. Mary asks, "How can this be?" With our knowledge of biology, some contemporary thinkers have asked the same. How was Mary's egg fertilized? In essence, that modern question is simply a more precise way of asking Mary's question, "How can this be?" The angel does not go into an excursus on pregnancy in the ancient world. Instead, the angel tells Mary that the power of the Most High will overshadow her. This is Luke's way of saying what Matthew also says: Jesus is son of God, and son of Mary.

Both Luke and Matthew make it clear that Mary was a virgin when she conceived and gave birth to Jesus. Later tradition goes further in stating that Mary was "ever virgin," though it should be recognized that the creed itself does not say that. However, each Sunday millions of Catholics today pray in the penitential rite of the Mass, the Confiteor "I confess":

> *I confess to almighty God,*
>> *and to you, my brothers and sisters,*
>> *that I have sinned through my own fault, in my thoughts and in*
>>> *my words,*
>> *in what I have done, and what I have failed to do.*
>> *Therefore I ask blessed Mary ever virgin,*
>> *all the angels and saints,*
>> *and you, my brothers and sisters,*
>> *to pray for me to the Lord our God.*[22]

The Confiteor as we have it today (and certainly in its pre-Vatican II form) is much later than the Apostles' Creed. The reference to the "ever Virgin" Mary, or her perpetual virginity, is a theological idea whose origins go back to Epiphanius and Jerome. Both the New Testament and the Apostles' Creed say that Mary was a virgin when she gave birth (Matt 1:25).

God-Man/ Man-God

Before the gospels were composed, Paul wrote letters. In his most famous letter, that to the Romans, Paul employs a creedal fragment[23] in a rhetorical flourish about God's Son,

descended from David according to the flesh, but established as Son of God in power according to the spirit of holiness through resurrection from the dead, Jesus Christ our Lord. (Rom 1:3-4).

We can see the parallel structure of this early creedal statement more clearly if we display it as such:

descended from David according to the flesh, but

established as Son of God in power according to the spirit of holiness
> *through resurrection from the dead, Jesus Christ our Lord*

The creedal fragment expresses a fundamental belief about Jesus. That is, he is descended from David according to the flesh (human), and he was declared to be Son of God by resurrection from the dead (divine). There is much more we could say about this early creed. At this point we see that it expresses what we would say is both the humanity and the divinity of Jesus. For the Synoptic Gospel writers, Jesus is son of Mary. His humanity is not in doubt. For Paul (who never mentions the mother of Jesus) Jesus is descended from David according to the flesh. His humanity is not in doubt. Many of the early Christians were struggling to show that Jesus is also divine. The marriage of humanity and divinity in the one person of Jesus was expressed in a variety of ways in the New Testament.

The Apostolic Fathers also wrestled with this mystery. For example, Ignatius of Antioch, who wrote seven letters to Christian churches on his way to martyrdom at Rome, says,

There is only one physician, who is both flesh and spirit, born and unborn, God in man, true life in death, both from Mary and from God, first subject to suffering and then beyond it, Jesus Christ our Lord.[24]

Commentators on Ignatius have recognized that, "When Ignatius refers to Christ as 'both fleshly and spiritual' (*Eph* 7.2; cf. *Sm.* 3.3), he has in mind the union of the divine and human in the God-Man and thus anticipates the classical two-nature christology."[25]

Many people today seem to be hidden docetists. Docetism was an early heresy that stressed the divinity of Jesus to the detriment of his humanity. Today many Christians may sympathize with this heresy in believing Jesus was fully divine, but not really accepting that he was fully human. Even though we say the words (in the Nicene Creed) "fully divine and fully human," it is difficult to unpack their meaning and appropriate application. For example, since Jesus was fully human, he had to grow in wisdom and knowledge (Luke 2:40). That means among other things, that he learned how to speak. He learned how to read. He made mistakes and learned from his mistakes. Yet, he did not sin (Heb 4:15). Sometimes modern Christians have the idea that Jesus was almost a divine actor on the stage, fully aware of everything around him so that he did not have to learn anything. However, if this were the case, Jesus would not have been fully human, for that is not the way human beings are.

On the other hand, there are some Christians who stress the humanity of Jesus to such a point that they seem to deny or even delay Jesus' divinity. For example, adoptianists (from the Latin term *adoptiani*) claimed that Jesus was a human being who was adopted by God because of his good deeds and merits.

In the Apostles' Creed, the article stating that he was conceived by the power of the Holy Spirit expresses his filial relationship with God, his divinity. Jesus incarnated God. Jesus fully expressed the love of God in the world in a way that nobody else could, for he and the Father are one. To say that he was born of Mary expresses his humanity. Jesus incarnated humanity and fully expressed what it means to be human. He was one with humanity.

The person of Jesus as divine and human is one of the central mysteries of Christian faith. Mystery in this sense does not mean, "Nobody will ever fully understand this so I won't think about it." Mystery instead means that no matter how fully we plumb the depths, there is always more to learn, more to ponder. Thus we say that the universe is a mystery. The more we understand about the universe, the more we realize that we understand very little about it. We will never exhaust the mysteries of the universe. That does not mean that we do not think about the mysteries of the universe. Quite the contrary, we think about its mysteries and ponder them often. So it is with the person of Christ. As we ponder Jesus, we will not exhaust him, but he will exhaust us. We will continue to approach him anew, and learn more. The fundamental mystery of the person of Jesus and his divine nature and human nature are expressed in this one article of faith.

Thus, this article reflects New Testament faith, as expressed particularly in Matthew, in Luke, and in Paul.

Summary

Jesus' relationship with God, his unique relationship of being son is expressed by his conception. Jesus was not conceived by normal marital relations. Rather, he was conceived by the power of the Holy Spirit, the dynamic presence of God in the world. Still, Jesus was born in the natural way of a woman, a virgin named Mary. Her virginity at the time of his birth gives testimony to his conception by the Holy Spirit.

DISCUSSION QUESTIONS
cf. CCC §456-570

1. What does it mean for humanity that Jesus is divine?
2. What does it mean for humanity that Jesus is human?
3. What are the times in your spiritual life when you tend to focus on Jesus' humanity?
4. What are the times in your spiritual life when you tend to focus on Jesus' divinity?
5. What scripture passages might you cite to demonstrate that Jesus was fully human?
6. What scripture passages might you cite to demonstrate that Jesus was fully divine?

Article

IV

He suffered
under Pontius
Pilate, was
crucified, died,
and was buried.

Article 4. He suffered under Pontius Pilate, was crucified, died, and was buried.

This article again situates the person of Jesus in history and moves from the conception and birth of Jesus to his suffering and death. There is no mention of his earthly ministry, his teaching, healing, or prophetic acts. Instead, we move immediately to the Paschal mystery, the suffering, death, burial and ultimate resurrection of Christ.

Jesus suffered

The article clearly states that Jesus suffered. The Greek verb "to suffer" is *paschein*. The Latin noun form is *passio*, from which the English term "passion" is derived. So the passion of Jesus is his suffering. The fact that Jesus suffered is present in the New Testament in the synoptic gospels (Matt 17:12; Mark 8:31; Luke 22:15) and in Heb 2:18; 5:8; 2 Cor 1:5; and many other passages. The suffering, death, and crucifixion of Jesus were undeniable, and had to be explained theologically by the early Christians.

The suffering servant songs of Isaiah (42:1-4; 49:1-7; 50:4-11; 52:13-53:12) became one interpretive key for understanding the suffering of Jesus. That is, God uses the suffering of his servant to justify the many (cf. Isa 53:11-12). This is certainly the way 1 Peter understands it, for 1 Pet 2:22 quotes Isa 53:9 explicitly before alluding to other Isaiah passages in the following verses (1 Pet 2:23-25). 1 Pet 2:21 states clearly that "Christ suffered for you," and says again in 1 Pet 3:18 "Christ suffered for sins." *1 Clement* 16 quotes Isaiah 53 at length.

The fact that Jesus suffered is certainly an article of faith, as we see from the Apostles' Creed. Still, it is possible to proclaim the message of Jesus without an over-emphasis on suffering. For example, the term suffering never appears in the Gospel of John with respect to Jesus or anyone else. Certainly in the Gospel of John Jesus does not suffer. There is not even an agony in the garden. Instead, the garden is the scene for the prayer of Jesus for the unity of his disciples, the coming of the spirit, the teaching on the vine and branches, and other vignettes. In the Gospel of John Jesus is crucified, but it is more akin to being raised in glory than suffering (John 3:14; 12:32; 21:19). This reminds us that although Jesus' suffering is an article of faith, Christianity can also emphasize Christ's glory vis-à-vis the suffering.

Pontius Pilate

Even so, Jesus suffered at the hands of the Roman authority Pontius Pilate, as each of the gospels, the Acts of the Apostles, and even 1 Tim 6:13 indicate. There is extrabiblical evidence that shows Pilate was the procurator of Judea from AD 26-36.[26] Judea was an imperial province rather than a senatorial province. Thus, the procurator was the vicar of the emperor, with full executive and judicial powers. That is, he enforced Roman law and acted as judge in the province.

As an occupying power, the Romans reserved the right to administer capital punishment to themselves (cf. Josephus, *Jewish Wars* 2.8.1; John 8:31). This fact is significant for the dating of Stephen's martyrdom (Acts 7:54-60). Acts tells us that Stephen was stoned by the high priest and council. We may surmise that it was only in the absence of a Roman prefect (during the time between Pilate's departure in A.D. 36 and the naming of the next prefect, Marcellus)[27] would the council feel free enough to inflict capital punishment on their own.

Though some New Testament texts portray Pilate as hesitant, extrabiblical texts show us that Pilate did not hesitate to execute hundreds of people at a time (Josephus, *Jewish Antiquities*, 18.3.2; 18.4.1). Indeed it was because of the ruthless nature of Pilate that he was eventually called back to Rome in A.D. 36 (Josephus, *Jewish Antiquities*, 18.4.2; Philo, *Embassy to Gaius*, 38).

So why do some New Testament authors portray Pilate as hesitant? For example, Mark claims that the Sanhedrin were guilty of having condemned Jesus (10:33; 14:64), even though it was Pilate who handed him over to death (15:15) without reason to accuse him (15:14). Moreover, Matthew says that Pilate was reluctant to take responsibility for Jesus' death (27:24), to which "all the people" responded, "his blood be on us and on our children" (27:25). It seems that the New Testament authors were attempting to affix blame for Jesus' death on the Jews rather than on the Romans, who had the power to execute. Of course, by the time Luke, Matthew, and John were writing, perhaps even Mark, the city of Jerusalem and the Jerusalem temple had already been destroyed by the Romans. As the Catholic Church teaches,

> ...the Gospel of Matthew reflects a situation of tension and even opposition between the two communities [Christians and Jews]. In it Jesus foresees that his disciples will be flogged in the synagogues and pursued from town to town (23:34). Matthew therefore is concerned to provide for the Christians' defense. Since that situation has radically changed, Matthew's polemic need no longer interfere with relations between Christians and Jews, and the aspect of continuity, can and ought to prevail. It is equally necessary to say this in relation to the destruction of the city and the Temple. This downfall is an event of the past which henceforth ought to evoke only deep compassion.[28]

Thus, the gospel writers, coming from their perspective vis-à-vis some Jews of their day, were (among other things) explaining theologically the destruction of the Temple, the mission to the Gentiles, and the resistance that many Jews had to the Christian message. In the passion narratives then, it was convenient to affix blame on the Jewish leaders, the Sanhedrin, and the crowds, rather than Pilate himself who ultimately held the power to inflict capital punishment. Indeed, even as Mark tells it, the fact that Pilate recognized Jesus as innocent but allowed him to be crucified, does not speak well for Roman justice, or Pilate's character.

Crucifixion

Jesus not only suffered at the hands of Pilate but he was also crucified. The term 'crucify' literally means 'to make a cross.' This form of capital punishment originated in Persia, but was perfected by the Romans. It was a rather common form of public execution.

One of the most famous examples of crucifixion might be Spartacus and the slave rebellion in the first century B.C. Spartacus led a rebellion of slaves over 120,000 strong. When the Romans finally put down the rebellion, an ancient authority tells us they crucified 6000 survivors along the Via Appia, the road that runs from Rome to Capua.[29] (Incidentally, according to Acts 28:13-16, this is the same road that Paul took into Rome.) You may have seen the 1960 Stanley Kubrick film *Spartacus* starring Kirk Douglas, Laurence Olivier, and Jean Simmons, that depicts the crucifixion of Spartacus and the other rebellious slaves along the Via Appia.

Crucifixion was not only public execution, but public humiliation, as the person was left to hang (usually naked) until death by asphyxiation, thirst, or exposure to the elements.

Often times Christians today do not reflect on the humiliation that accompanied this form of execution, focusing instead on the suffering, or how much it hurt. Yet, the humility and humiliation of Jesus was part of the early Christian message (Phil 2:7-8; cf. Acts 8:33).

Death by crucifixion was also significant in that Jesus' followers hailed him as the Messiah, "king of Israel" as he entered Jerusalem (John 12:13). Thus the sign was placed over the cross in a mocking tone, "Jesus of Nazareth King of the Jews" (John 19:19). It is as though the Romans were mocking not only Jesus but those who had hailed his entry into Jerusalem.

Furthermore, in the book of Deuteronomy we find this intriguing passage:

*"If a man guilty of a capital offense is put to death
and his corpse hung on a tree, it shall not remain on
the tree overnight. You shall bury it the same day;
otherwise, since God's curse rests on him who hangs
on a tree, you will defile the land which the LORD, your
God, is giving you as an inheritance. (Deut 21:22-23).*

Thus, one crucified (for this is how the passage was
applied in the first century AD) was thereby cursed by God.
What better way to demonstrate that Jesus was NOT the
messiah but to crucify him, that is, hang him from a tree
thereby showing he is cursed by God. A cursed messiah is a
contradiction. A crucified Jesus then becomes a theological
dilemma. How can this person be the Messiah? The Messiah
is to be king of Israel, restoring independence to the land like
King David. The Messiah is not to be crucified, much less
suffer. In fact, nowhere in the Old Testament does it state
that the Messiah would suffer. Isaiah speaks of a suffering
servant, but not a suffering Messiah.[30] Paul knew well the
theological quandary he faced:

*For Jews demand signs and Greeks look for wisdom,
but we proclaim Christ crucified, a stumbling block to
Jews and foolishness to Gentiles, but to those who are
called, Jews and Greeks alike, Christ the power of God
and the wisdom of God. For the foolishness of God is
wiser than human wisdom, and the weakness of God is
stronger than human strength. (1 Cor 1:22-25).*

We now hear Paul in a new light when he says, we preach
Christ (the Messiah) crucified, a stumbling block to Jews and
folly to the Greeks. Why is this a stumbling block? Precisely
because crucifixion means cursed by God, and Messiah
means anointed by God. This is a stumbling block because a
crucified Messiah goes against the plain sense of scripture.
The Greeks consider this folly. Paul for his part recognizes in
this crucified Messiah the plan of God. God's wisdom looks
foolish. God's power looks weak, a stumbling block.

Paul also wrestles with Deut 21:13 in his letter to the
Galatians. Paul believes that the law places humanity under
a curse. Yet, Christ dying the way he did (by crucifixion),
became accursed and thereby took upon himself the curse of

the law. When he died, so did the law. Now, by means of his death and resurrection a right relationship with God is based not on external observance of Mosaic Law, but on life in the Spirit that flows from faith in Jesus Christ. A right relationship with God is no longer limited to Jews, but is now extended to all humanity, Jew and Greek alike (cf. Gal 3:13-14).

Paul then truly grappled with this mystery of faith: a crucified Messiah. At times we may simply express faith in Jesus Christ crucified, without appreciating how incompatible this is with a plain reading of the Old Testament. Our faith is built on the faith of the apostles. Paul for one did much to demonstrate that a crucified Messiah actually expresses the plan of God rather than contradicts it.

Sometimes Christians have the idea that the Old Testament was something of a script, and Jesus perfectly played the role of Messiah. Only a stubborn fool could not have seen that. Why then could the Jews not have seen it? The argument would continue by saying they were stubborn, hard-headed, blind to God, or bore some other negative trait. It is important to recall the words of the 2002 Pontifical Biblical Commission document, "The Jewish People and their Sacred Scripture in the Christian Bible," quoted above in the commentary on article 2, which says,

> *Christian faith recognises the fulfilment, in Christ, of the Scriptures and the hopes of Israel, but it does not understand this fulfilment as a literal one. Such a conception would be reductionist. In reality, in the mystery of Christ crucified and risen, fulfilment is brought about in a manner unforeseen. It includes transcendence. Jesus is not confined to playing an already fixed role — that of Messiah — but he confers, on the notions of Messiah and salvation, a fullness which could not have been imagined in advance; he fills them with a new reality; one can even speak in this connection of a "new creation". It would be wrong to consider the prophecies of the Old Testament as some kind of photographic anticipations of future events. All the texts, including those which later were read as messianic prophecies, already had an immediate import and meaning for their contemporaries before*

attaining a fuller meaning for future hearers. The
messiahship of Jesus has a meaning that is new and
original.[31]

Yet, in the creed we recite that Jesus is the Messiah; he
suffered; he was crucified; and he died. It is significant that
the creed states that Jesus died. There were early schisms
based on this point alone. Some could admit that Jesus was
crucified but they would not claim that he died. Indeed, this is
one point over which Muslims and Christians disagree today.
The Koran states that ....

Jesus died

> *And their saying: Surely we have killed the Messiah,*
> *Isa son of Marium [Jesus son of Mary], the apostle of*
> *Allah; and they did not kill him nor did they crucify him,*
> *but it appeared to them so (like Isa) and most surely*
> *those who differ therein are only in a doubt about it;*
> *they have no knowledge respecting it, but only follow a*
> *conjecture, and they killed him not for sure. [4.157]* [32]

For Christians, the burial confirms the death. That is, we
don't bury people who are alive. We bury the dead. To say
that Jesus was buried is akin to underlining the fact that he
died.

This article of faith reflects the even more ancient
articulation by Paul in the fifteenth chapter of 1 Corinthians
wherein he recalls what was handed on to him:

> *For I handed on to you as of first importance what*
> *I also received: that Christ died for our sins in*
> *accordance with the scriptures; that he was buried;*
> *that he was raised on the third day in accordance with*
> *the scriptures; that he appeared to Cephas, then to the*
> *Twelve. (1 Cor 15:3-5).*

If we arrange this early Christian creed according to its
four "that" statements we can see clearly that the second
and the fourth statements confirm the first and the third
respectively.

> *that Christ died for our sins in accordance with the*
> *scriptures;*

> *that he was buried;*

that he was raised on the third day in accordance with the scriptures;

that he appeared to Cephas, then to the Twelve

The burial confirms the death. That is, the statement that Christ was buried substantiates the claim that he died, much like the statement that he appeared to Cephas substantiates the claim that he was raised. Scholars generally agree that Paul wrote 1 Corinthians about AD 57. He preached to the Corinthians, in Corinth, about AD 51-52. It would have been at that time that he gave them this formula that he himself was given. When would he have received this? According to his own words he was in Jerusalem only twice before: once for fifteen days (ca. AD 36) and once more to attend the "Jerusalem Council" (ca. AD 50).[33] Perhaps he learned this early creed from the Jerusalem church at one of these visits. At any rate, the formula itself can be no later than AD 50, at most some 20 years after the death and resurrection of Jesus.

Ever since the death of Jesus, theologians and other Christians have been wrestling with that fact, and how to think about it theologically. Did Jesus HAVE TO die? Why was he crucified? Was this part of a grand plan, or is it simply how human beings reacted to Jesus? Various answers throughout history have focused primarily on the theory of atonement. That is, Jesus' death brought humanity to God according to a foreordained plan. In some way, Jesus' death appeased God. Or, God demanded the blood-sacrifice of his Son. While some of these theological ideas may stem from certain New Testament authors, contemporary theologians are questioning whether such ideas are germane to a twenty-first century audience. Does God truly demand the blood-sacrifice of his son? Is there really a divine plan that foresees each and every event? Are we all actors on a divine stage? Certainly many atheists are so precisely because of this notion of God. For example, Susan Jacoby wrote recently on the WashingtonPost.com weblog, "On Faith" that,

If there were a deity responsible for both human evil and impersonal natural disasters, I would hate him. I would prefer to go to hell rather than to make bargains

with such a cruel, capricious Master of the Universe.[34]

Rather than propose a God who is pleased with blood-sacrifice, or who interferes to stop some cases of moral evil and natural disaster but not others, a different way of theologizing about Christ's death may be this. Christ is the enfleshment, the embodiment of God's love in the world. What is the human response to incarnate divine love? Our response is misunderstanding, anger, hostility and violence to the point of murder. Ultimately, we kill it.

Despite our actions, God has another response which is to raise Jesus from the dead. God has the final word. Our cruel inhumanity to one another, our cruel inhumanity even to incarnate love, will not be overcome by the love of God, who raises even the dead to new life. Christian theologians will continue to plumb the depths of the death and resurrection of Jesus for meaning. This is not something we exhaust. The mystery of incarnate love exhausts us.

Summary

With a reputation for ruthlessness, Pontius Pilate was a historical figure who was the Roman governor of Judea. He was the authority under whom Jesus really suffered, was crucified, and died. Jesus then suffered capital punishment at the hands of the state. He truly died and was buried. In so doing, Jesus does not explain suffering and death, but gives meaning to it.

DISCUSSION QUESTIONS
cf. CCC §571-630

1. What is the proper relationship between faith and the governing power?

2. Where do I stand on the issue of capital punishment? Does the fact that Jesus died at the hands of the state make any difference?

3. Why did Jesus suffer?

4. How would Christian faith be different if we claimed that Jesus did not die?

Article

V

He descended
into hell. On the
third day he rose
again.

Article 5.   He descended into hell. On the third day he rose again.

This fifth article of the creed is in some sense two articles. (1) He descended into hell. (2) He rose on the third day. Perhaps one reason it states two articles is that the first, he descended into hell, (*descendit ad infernos*) is not in the earliest versions of the creed. Instead the earliest creeds simply stated that after Jesus died, he rose again on the third day.

Descent into hell

The absence of the phrase in the creed reflects the understanding of one of the earliest creeds of all, one that Paul cites to the Corinthians, and that we cited in the previous chapter.

> For I handed on to you as of first importance what
> I also received: that Christ died for our sins in
> accordance with the scriptures; that he was buried;
> that he was raised on the third day in accordance with
> the scriptures; that he appeared to Cephas, then to the
> Twelve. (1 Cor 15:3-5).

The absence of the phrase also seems to reflect the understanding that Luke gives us when he relates the conversation between the repentant thief and Jesus:

> Then he said, "Jesus, remember me when you
> come into your kingdom." He replied to him, "Amen,
> I say to you, today you will be with me in Paradise."
> (Luke 23:42-43)

Both the passage from Corinthians, and the passage from Luke show no awareness of a descent into hell. Rather, with Luke it seems that after his death Jesus' transit to the Father was immediate. Even in the Gospel of John (20:17) where Jesus says to Mary Magdalene, "Stop holding on to me, for I have not yet ascended to the Father," there is no mention of a descent into hell. The hymn Paul uses in Philippians also has no mention of hell, or even a descent to the dead (Phil 2:6-11). There is simply no New Testament evidence of Jesus' descending into hell after his death.[35] (1 Pet 3:19 is a special case, addressed below).

Indeed, this claim that Christ descended into hell is not even in the earliest versions of the Apostles' Creed. For example, Rufinus, commenting on the creed from Aquilea (cited above) said, "In the creed of the Roman church, we should notice, the words DESCENDED TO HELL are not added, nor for that matter does the clause feature in the Eastern churches."[36] We recall that the phrase is not in the baptismal creed from Hippolytus either.

In fact, this creed from Aquilea seems to be the earliest evidence we find for the phrase being added. The phrase in Latin is "*descendit ad inferna*" translated as "he descended into hell." The Latin term "*inferna*" literally means "lower parts" but could also mean the place of the damned. Other Latin texts read "*descendit ad inferos*" which means "he descended to the departed." Thus, for the early church the phrase would have conjured up images of the abode of the dead, and only later a fiery hell. The abode of the dead in the lower parts of the world is conveyed by the Hebrew term *sheol*, often translated as *hades* in Greek. The idea of a fiery judgment, or fiery hell was expressed in the New Testament by the Greek transliteration of the Hebrew term *gehenna*. See the comments on article 12 (page 98) for more about *sheol* and its background.

The Greek term *gehenna* is ultimately a shortened form of *gê-hinnōm* which means Valley of Hinnom. This valley marked the northern border of Judah after the return from the Babylonian exile (Neh 11:30). It was the site of child sacrifice, practiced by certain Judeans not the least of which was the king! (2 Kgs 16:3; 21:6; 2 Chr 28:3; 33:6) There were so many Judeans killed in this valley in the war with the Babylonians, that Jeremiah proclaims that the valley will heretofore be known as the valley of slaughter (Jer 7:29-34; 19:1-5). In the New Testament the term *gehenna* and other corresponding terms such as "lake of fire and sulphur" describe primarily the fate of the wicked, the devil, and the devil's angels[37] (Matt 25:41; Rev 20:10,15; 21:18). Still, *hades* and *gehenna* are distinct, with *hades* representing the abode of the dead and *gehenna* representing the abode of the damned.[38]

So, what are we to make of this phrase, descended to hell? Why was it inserted into the creed in the first place? The ancient mind understood the world differently than we do today. For example, in general one believed that there was heaven (above the earth), the earth, and the region(s) under the earth. God reigned in heaven. Human beings were on the earth. The dead were in the lower regions of the earth. There are New Testament echos of this popular cosmology. For example, Eph 4:9-10 and Phil 2:10.

There was a belief expressed by many Apostolic Fathers that Christ descended to the dead after his own death. Though not explicitly stated in the New Testament, there are passages that lent themselves to this understanding. For example, on Jesus' lips in the Gospel of Matthew is this statement, "Just as Jonah was in the belly of the whale three days and three nights, so will the Son of Man be in the heart of the earth three days and three nights." (Matt 12:40). Thus, some Apostolic Fathers articulate a belief in Christ's descent to the dead, for example Ignatius (*Mag.* 9) and Polycarp (*Phil.* 1).

But it was Irenaeus (ca. 125-200) who said explicitly that Jesus preached to the departed while he was there.

And on account of this the Lord descended into the places which are under the earth and proclaimed to them the good news of his coming, which is the remission of sins received by those who believe in him.[39]

Tertullian (ca. 150-230) echoes this belief (*De Anima*, 55) as does Clement of Alexandria (ca. 150-216). Yet none of these explicitly cite 1 Pet 3:18-22 which says,

For Christ also suffered for sins once, the righteous for the sake of the unrighteous, that he might lead you to God. Put to death in the flesh, he was brought to life in the spirit. In it he also went to preach to the spirits in prison, who had once been disobedient while God patiently waited in the days of Noah during the building of the ark, in which a few persons, eight in all, were saved through water. This prefigured baptism, which saves you now. It is not a removal of dirt from the body but an appeal to God for a clear conscience, through the resurrection of Jesus Christ, who has gone into heaven and is at the right hand of God, with angels, authorities, and powers subject to him. (1 Pet 3:18-22).

Origen does cite this passage explicitly to say that Christ's preaching to those who perished in the deluge is an example of the wicked who could be saved (*On Principles.* 2.5.3). In the end, most church fathers do not tie this passage to Christ's descent into hell. That thinking develops much later. Instead, the two traditions/thoughts developed independently. Even Augustine wrestled with the proper way to integrate the scripture passage with the doctrine of descent into hell (Letter 164, to Evodius). Today of course, the church uses 1 Pet 3:19 in support of its teaching that Christ descended into hell (CCC §632) and in that way the doctrine might be an example of the *sensus plenior* (more full sense) of the scriptural passage.

In summary, the New Testament itself has no direct claim of Christ's descent to the dead, much less a descent into hell. In fact, this latter claim is not in the earliest versions of the creed (e.g., Rufinus and Hippolytus), but is present in the creed of Aquilea. Though Clement was the first to allude to the scriptural passage of 1 Pet 3:19 in the context of descent into hell, even that allusion is not explicit.

Prescinding from the history of theology, we must ask ourselves, "What did the scriptural passage mean when the ink was wet?" Modern scholars maintain that the 1 Peter passage is not about Christ's descent into the dead, much less a descent into hell. For example, in a recent commentary on 1 Peter, John Elliott states clearly,

The "disobedient spirits in prison" are not deceased humans but the angelic spirits whose disobedience led to the destruction through the Flood, and Christ's announcement entails a confirmation of their eternal condemnation and confinement. The subsequent development of the descensus theory and its theological interests should not be allowed to determine or obscure the meaning of 1 Pet 3:19 in its original historical, literary, or theological context.[40]

In fact, Elliott correctly points out that the 1 Peter passage never mentions a descent. Instead, he maintains that the passage in question refers instead to Christ's ascent into heaven (which it does say in v.22). The doctrine of Christ's descent into hell then arose independently from this scriptural passage. Not until the time of Augustine was this link cemented for later theology.

The "infernal" language in this article speaks to its own world-view. Imagine for a moment the cosmology envisioned. Heaven, earth, and under the earth (cf. Phil 2:10). Heaven is above the earth, and hell is below it. Yet, do any of us in a post-modern scientific, space-faring age accept this cosmology? We invariably, perhaps unconsciously, recognize that it is speaking to the realm of myth, of metaphor. Hell is not truly down there. Instead, down below the earth's crust we have the mantle, and eventually the core. Indeed, if we were to drill down far enough we would come to the other side of the earth, for earth is a sphere. We know that today without even thinking about it. It is a part of our unconscious world-view. In the same way, heaven is not up there. Up there the atmosphere becomes thinner. The pull of gravity becomes weaker and we enter the exosphere, outer space.

The verbiage seems to be a claim for the atemporal aspect of Christ's death. That is, the benefits of Christ's death are not limited to those who live after the time of Christ. Christ's death has salvific import on those who were born before Christ. That is, Christ's death and subsequent descent into hell opened heaven for all. Catechetically, this was often portrayed in images such as Adam's sin locked the gates of heaven. Thus, all humanity from Adam to Christ was locked out of heaven. When Christ came, he descended into hell, brought up all those denied entrance into heaven, and then opened the gates of heaven for all (cf. CCC § 637). Of course, we recognize that these images and ideas emerged from theological speculation, presented in imaginary terms to solve the theological puzzle of the destiny of human beings before Christ.

No less an authority than the late John Paul II recognized this when he said:

> The word of the Gospel and of the Cross reaches all, even those belonging to the most distant past generations; because all who have been saved have been made participants in the Redemption, even before the historical event of Christ's sacrifice on Golgotha happened. ...This is the "truth" drawn from the biblical texts cited and which is expressed in the article of the Creed that speaks of "descent into hell."[41]

This understanding is also echoed in the *US Catholic Catechism for Adults*, "In the language of the early church, this [Jesus descended into hell] meant that Jesus went into the realm of the dead, from which he called out all just people who had lived before him to enter with him into the glory of the Kingdom of Heaven."[42]

We might ask ourselves how we solve the theological puzzles of our own day. Often times we hear the perennial question: "what happens to the indigenous person in the deepest forests of the East Asian Pacific Islands who has never heard of Christ?" How do we answer that question? What about all those who have died without ever hearing the name of Jesus? Are they saved? We might think of Christ's descent into hell as the early Church's response to these kinds of questions. Even if some modern people might object to the notion of hell and Christ's descent into it, we may recognize that these are metaphorical images used to convey the theological truth that Christ's death has a salvific effect for all humanity.

As mentioned above, Paul recited what he learned. He received this statement of faith and in turn handed it on the Corinthians. Thus, this article of faith, that Jesus rose again on the third day, is certainly of demonstrable apostolic origin.

The statement of faith from 1 Corinthians, as well as the Apostles' Creed has language so familiar sometimes we do not think about it thoroughly. For example, each states that Jesus rose "on the third day." But what precisely does that mean? Though the synoptic gospels do not agree with the gospel of John about the date of Jesus death, they all agree that the last supper was a Thursday, Jesus was crucified on a Friday, and the empty tomb was discovered on a Sunday, the day on which one or more resurrection appearances took place, depending on which gospel we read. In the end however, neither the earliest creeds nor the Pauline creeds state the day Jesus died. Instead, they are content to say that he rose "on the third day."

Thus, homilists in counting the three days count Friday (the day Jesus died), Saturday, and Easter Sunday is the third day. However, it would be more accurate to say that the *empty tomb was first discovered* on the third day, or on Easter Sunday, the first day of the week (John 20:1). Did anybody truly witness Jesus being raised? No. Instead, the third day, Easter Sunday, was the day the disciples discovered the empty tomb, and first witnessed the risen Christ. As to when Jesus rose, we have no eyewitness testimony.

We imagine that early Christians perhaps lamented the fact that there was no description of the resurrection itself. Thus, we have the apocryphal *Gospel of Peter*. The precise dating of the *Gospel of Peter* is a matter of some debate. For our purposes we consider it spurious and later than the canonical gospels, expressing a rather docetic view of Jesus (stressing his divinity over his humanity), and a rather imaginative view of the resurrection, told in this way:

> *9:35 But in the night in which the Lord's Day dawned,*
> *when the soldiers were safeguarding (it) two by two in*

Jesus rose

*every watch, there was a loud voice in heaven; 9:36
and they saw that the heavens were opened and that
two males who had much radiance had come down
from there and come near the sepulcher. 9:37 But that
stone which had been thrust against the door, having
rolled by itself, went a distance off the side; and the
sepulcher opened, and both the young men entered.
10:38 And so those soldiers, having seen, awakened
the centurion and the elders (for they too were present,
safeguarding). 10:39 And while they were relating what
they had seen, again they see three males who have
come out from they sepulcher, with the two supporting
the other one, and a cross following them, 10:40 and
the head of the two reaching unto heaven, but that of
the one being led out by hand by them going beyond
the heavens. 10:41 And they were hearing a voice from
the heavens saying, "Have you made proclamation to
the fallen-asleep?" 10:42 And an obeisance was heard
from the cross, "Yes."*[43]

This is obviously fanciful Christian imagination. The point remains. There is no canonical description of the resurrection itself, only the discovery of the tomb on the first day of the week (Mark 16:1-2; Matt 28:1; Luke 24:1; John 20:1). Or, we have predictions and mentions by various people about Jesus rising on the third day (Matt. 16:21; 17:23; 20:19; Luke 9:22; 18:33; 24:7,21,46) or after three days (Matt. 12:40; 27:63; Mark 8:31; 9:31; 10:34). There are faith statements that God raised Jesus, or Jesus was raised on the third day (Acts 10:40; 1 Cor 15:4). In Matthew, the soldiers are ordered to secure the tomb until the third day, lest his disciples come and steal the body (27:64). There is a Lucan story in which Jesus says, "and on the third day I accomplish my purpose" (13:32). And of course there are the temple predictions, seen in light of resurrection, "Destroy this temple and in three days I will raise it up" (cf. Matt. 26:61; 27:40; Mark 14:58; 15:29; John 2:19). But perhaps nowhere is the claim so bold as in Luke 24:46, "Thus it is written that the Messiah would suffer and rise from the dead on the third day." The Pauline creed cited above also adds the intriguing phrase, "according to the scriptures."

We may ask, where does it say in the scriptures that the Messiah would rise on the third day, much less suffer (see comments on article 4)? The short answer is that it does not. Nowhere in the Old Testament is there any mention of rising on the third day by the Messiah or anyone else. It seems Christians however, read Hosea 6:1-2 in this light.

Come, let us return to the LORD, For it is he who has rent, but he will heal us; he has struck us, but he will bind our wounds. He will revive us after two days; on the third day he will raise us up, to live in his presence. (Hosea 6:1-2).

I say "seems" because there is no direct evidence citing this passage in the New Testament. The New Testament authors were content to say that Jesus rose on the third day "according to the Scriptures" without citing any particular scripture passage. By making this claim, they were able to maintain that the resurrection of Jesus fulfilled scripture, and thus was according to the plan of God.

Resurrection, or Jesus' rising from the dead, is perhaps the central tenet of Christianity. Had the apostles not proclaimed that Jesus rose from the dead, Jesus would have been understood as perhaps a good teacher who met a violent end. As it stands, the apostles proclaimed the Easter message, "The Lord has truly been raised" (Luke 24:34). "I have seen the Lord" (John 20:18,25; 1 Cor 9:1). This apostolic preaching formed the basis of the church. As Paul tells the Corinthians, "Therefore, whether it be I or they, so we preach and so you believed." (1 Cor 15:11). And thus it has continued through the centuries. The Easter message is proclaimed anew each Easter Sunday, each weekly Sunday, indeed each day of the year. "So we preach and so you believed." Because the apostles believed and preached, we too believe and preach.

Recently there have been headlines about the supposed tomb of Jesus being found, perhaps containing the bones of Jesus himself. I am often asked what I think of this "discovery." I usually respond by saying that it depends not on what I think of this claim, but what would the apostles have thought had the bones of Jesus been in an ossuary in

Jerusalem? In so responding, I attempt to draw attention to the fact that ours is an apostolic faith. That is, our faith is built on the faith of the apostles. The apostles believed that Jesus rose from the dead. Would their belief have been so strong had Jesus' bones been in an ossuary not a few miles away?

Indeed, in the Gospel of Matthew we sense an apologetic motif creeping in when we hear the story of Pilate stationing guards lest the disciples steal the body and claim that Jesus rose (Matt 27:62-66). If at the time of the apostles' preaching, there were an ossuary containing Jesus' bones, one could deny the Easter message simply by pointing to those same bones. As the story goes, the tomb was empty, and the apostles proclaimed that Jesus rose. Faith or unbelief is the response.

We believe and are Christian, or we do not believe, and are therefore not Christian. Or perhaps like Thomas we say, "Unless I see the mark of the nails in his hands and put my finger into the nailmarks and put my hand into his side, I will not believe." (John 20:25). Truly some early Christians shared this sentiment for the evangelist records these words on the lips of Jesus, "Blessed are those who have not seen and have believed." (John 20:29b).

> *"how can some among you say there is no resurrection of the dead? If there is no resurrection of the dead, then neither has Christ been raised. And if Christ has not been raised, then empty (too) is our preaching; empty, too, your faith." (1 Cor 15:12b-14).*

Clearly, not all Christians could accept the resurrection. Even 2 Timothy mentions a "Hymenaeus and Philetus, who have deviated from the truth by saying that (the) resurrection has already taken place and are upsetting the faith of some." (2 Tim 2:17b-18).

Maybe the same challenges that faced the early Christians face us. Claims that the disciples stole the body of Jesus, the reluctant faith of Thomas, or a denial of the resurrection altogether, are all evidenced in the New Testament, indeed, even in our own day. Paul could give no demonstrable proof of the resurrection of Jesus other than his own eyewitness testimony, and the reports about the eyewitness testimony of others (1 Cor 15:3-8). Ultimately, the same "proof" offered to the Corinthians is offered to us today. The apostolic preaching "I have seen the Lord" engages us. We cannot see the Lord as the apostles did. But we can listen to the preaching of the apostles and choose to believe or not. This is the same option given to the first generation of Christians at Corinth. The choice that faced them faces us.

Christ's death had atemporal aspects in that it released all from the power of death. Salvation is now available to all, regardless of time and space. Christ's resurrection was God's definitive affirmation of Jesus Christ. By the resurrection, Jesus conquered death once and for all, and gave humanity a glimpse into the future that awaits us. The resurrection of Christ remains a central tenet of Christianity.

Summary

DISCUSSION QUESTIONS
cf. CCC §631-658

1. Where is the risen Christ now?
2. Why does it matter that Jesus rose from the dead?
3. Though the creed says he rose from the dead, many New Testament passages say that God raised Jesus from the dead. What's the difference? Why does it matter?
4. What does Christ's descent into hell mean for contemporary Christians?

Article

VI

He ascended
into heaven and
is seated at the
right hand of the
Father.

Article 6.   He ascended into heaven and is seated at the right hand of the Father.

The previous chapter recognized that the article of faith used metaphorical language of Christ's descent into hell to teach that salvation is available to all. Now in this article we read more metaphorical language speaking of Christ's ascent into heaven. One difference between the descent into hell and the ascent into heaven is that the latter expression finds its roots in the New Testament, especially Luke (24:50-53), Luke's second volume, Acts of the Apostles (1:6-12), and John (20:17).

Old Testament

The Old Testament provides a rich background for understanding the concept of ascension into heaven, which essentially means ascension to the realm of God. For example, Enoch is said to have walked with God (Gen 5:24) and Elijah is taken to heaven in a fiery chariot (2 Kings 2:1-18). Coronation psalms speak of the king being seated at the right hand of God (24, 47, 68, esp. 110, cf. also 118) and so serve as a background to understanding ascension language. In ancient cultures the one seated on the right of the host enjoyed special favor. Thus, to be seated at God's right means to enjoy the favor and power of God as the psalm indicates. In the Old Testament, the king was said to enjoy this special favor of God.

New Testament

The New Testament ascension stories of Jesus confirm the resurrection appearance stories in as much as they combine both into one. The ascension of Jesus is the final leave-taking before his assembled followers. After his ascension Jesus will no longer appear to his disciples as he once did. The ascension in effect answers the believer's question, where is the risen Lord now? The answer is that he has ascended to heaven.

Only Luke in his gospel and in Acts gives us a narrative of the ascension of Jesus. Other New Testament authors simply assume it, or make some reference to it. For example, the great Christological hymn of Philippians speaks simply of the exaltation of Christ (2:9). 1 Pet 3:22 mentions Christ "gone into heaven." 1 Tim 3:16 expresses something similar in saying he was "taken up in glory."

Heaven itself is a metaphor for the other worldly presence or dwelling place of God. In antiquity the dwelling place of God was understood to be up. Thus if Jesus goes to God he ascends.

As this is metaphorical language, we recognize that the heavens are not really "up." We recall that the ancient mind understood the earth and the heavens differently than we do today. A careful reading of Genesis 1 tells us that there is a firmament, or dome in the sky separating the heavens from the earth (Psalm 19:2; Job 37:18). Above the dome is where God kept his storerooms for rain, ice, snow, etc. (Job 37:6; 38:22-23). The earth itself was thought to be a disk surrounded by the oceans. Of course, we don't understand the world in that way today. A literal reading of Genesis 1 would discourage a modern person from sending a rocket into outer space, for it would crash into the dome! Today, we have an entirely different cosmology.

Modern preconceptions

The modern understanding of the world recognizes the earth as a sphere, which rotates on its own axis (to give us day and night) and which revolves around the sun (to give us seasons, and years). Ancient Greek thinkers (as opposed to the biblical world-view) knew the earth was a sphere. For one, they had taken notice of the shadow of the earth when it passed over the moon during an eclipse. Also, having made precise measurements of shadows cast by the midday sun at different latitudes, they were able to determine the circumference of the earth's sphere.

Though the ancient Greeks understood the earth was a sphere, they did not believe it rotated on its own axis, or revolved around the sun. They had considered these as possibilities, but ultimately dismissed them for (at the time) good scientific reasons.[44]

Of course, today we take for granted that the earth is a sphere, rotates on its axis, and revolves around the sun. We travel in airplanes seven miles high, far above some clouds. We distinguish between the troposphere, the stratosphere, the mesosphere, the thermosphere, and the exosphere. Satellites travel through space in geosynchronous orbit. The moon itself is a satellite orbiting the earth. If we travel high enough with enough power we would not hit the dome imagined in Genesis 1, but we would escape earth's gravitational pull, and experience weightlessness, with the vast expanse of the universe all around us.

In fact, if one were to point straight up into the sky at any given time of the day, then point up again at the sky twelve hours later, that one would be pointing at different sides of the sky, completely different parts of the universe. In other words, noon at one point on the globe is a different sky than midnight at the same point on the globe. Only, the daytime sky with its bright sun obscures the stars we might see at that point. The ancient mind did not understand the world in this way.

What does it mean then for Christians to proclaim Christ's ascent into heaven? Some may ask, "How far up into the sky did he ultimately go?" "Did he go only so far up as to move beyond the ability of human vision, then vanish?" Such questions do not respect one fundamental point. We are expressing a theological truth by using metaphor.

Summary

Ascension into heaven means that Christ lives now with God, at his right hand, exalted to glory. Christ enjoys the favor of God, and shares in God's power.

DISCUSSION QUESTIONS
cf. CCC §659-667

1. What other metaphors might we use to express the same fundamental truth expressed by Jesus' ascension into heaven?

2. Given that Jesus shares in the power of God, how do you experience that power in your own life?

3. Did Jesus share in the power of God during his earthly life? If so, what is different about the heavenly power the risen Lord enjoys now?

Article

VII

He will come
again to judge
the living and the
dead.

Article 7. He will come again to judge the living and the dead.

To say that Jesus Christ, God's only Son, our Lord will come again presupposes that he came once already. It was clear to the early Christians that Jesus was humble in death. (Phil 2:7-8; cf. Acts 8:33). He was, as the prophet says, like the lamb led to the slaughter. However, the Jews of Jesus' day were expecting not a weak, submissive Messiah. The lamb led to the slaughter was the suffering servant. The Old Testament does not say the suffering servant and the Messiah were one and the same. Christians made that claim based on their experience of the risen Christ. The Lord Jesus, raised from the dead, shattered many preconceived notions and reset the deck so to speak. The Sacred Scriptures were read anew in light of the resurrection. The early Christians drew new connections heretofore unseen. Since Jesus was the Messiah, and he suffered and died on the cross, it was "easy" to make the connection of a suffering Messiah.

Jews of Jesus' day were generally expecting a Messiah who would be a powerful ruler, trampling foes, restoring the kingdom, and leading an age of peace. After the death and resurrection of Jesus his followers claimed that Jesus was in fact the Messiah who had come. Now, we can expect him to come AGAIN, only this time in power to judge the living and the dead. Jesus, the Lord himself would judge the people, bringing the righteous to live with him forever, and vanquishing the evil. Apocalyptic images were rampant (cf. Joel 3:12).

Christian belief in the coming again of Jesus Christ, the Lord, is ancient. In fact one of the prayers that Paul preserves for us in Aramaic is simply one word, *maranatha*, which means "Come, our lord" (1 Cor 16:22b). The Aramaic preserved by Paul gives scholars the idea that this monologue prayer had its setting in the early days of the post-resurrectional community, pre-dating Paul himself. Jesus died on the cross and in doing so did not act as judge. Yet, Christians believed that Jesus would return/appear and then act as judge of the living and the dead. (2 Tim 4:1,8; 1 Pet 4:5)

Old Testament

In the Old Testament, the power to judge was God's (e.g., 1 Sam 2:10; Psalm 96:10,13; 98:9; 110:6; Isa 33:22; Eze 7:27; 24:14; 35:11). Judgment was based on a person's actions. Often in biblical texts we hear the voice of those who are maltreated, or treated with injustice. For example, Amos (2:6-7; 4:1; 5:12; 8:4-6) decries the rich who gain their wealth on the backs of the poor. In these cases the oppressed have no one to turn to but God. God is said to have a concern for the poor, the widowed, and the orphan precisely because these people are often oppressed, without recourse to justice. Thus, God will act on their behalf, meting out justice, protecting the basic human rights of all.

New Testament

In the New Testament there are passages that state clearly that God will judge (e.g., Rom 3:6; 1 Pet 2:12; Heb 12:23) but there are others that recognize Jesus would have a role in that judgment. For example, Paul says that God through Jesus will judge the secret thoughts of all (Rom 2:16).[45] In many other New Testament passages the power to judge on the last day clearly belongs to Jesus. When he returns he will act as judge. For example, in the Gospel of Matthew Jesus describes the eschatological judgment with the image of separating sheep from goats. In this parable those who have treated the poor and outcast of the world with kindness and loving care are rewarded, for in so doing they were showing kindness and loving care to Jesus himself. On the other hand those who neglected the care of the poor were condemned for neglecting Jesus (Matt 25:31-46).

Judgment is, in fact, a strong New Testament theme that we don't discuss too often today. Perhaps it is the basis of judgment in the story that makes us shy away from the topic.

The fact that both the living and the dead will be judged conjures up images from 1 Thess 4:13-18 with the dead rising to meet the living Lord in the air (though in that passage there is no judgment), and the famous story of the parable of Lazarus, the rich man, in Luke.

> There was a rich man who dressed in purple garments and fine linen and dined sumptuously each day. And lying at his door was a poor man named Lazarus, covered with sores, who would gladly have eaten his fill of the scraps that fell from the rich man's table. Dogs even used to come and lick his sores. When the poor man died, he was carried away by angels to the bosom of Abraham. The rich man also died and was buried, and from the netherworld, where he was in torment, he raised his eyes and saw Abraham far off and Lazarus at his side. And he cried out, 'Father Abraham, have pity on me. Send Lazarus to dip the tip of his finger in water and cool my tongue, for I am suffering torment in these flames.' Abraham replied, 'My child, remember that you received what was good during your lifetime while Lazarus likewise received what was bad; but now he is comforted here, whereas you are tormented. (Luke 16:19-25).

In this story the roles are reversed (which is a typically Lucan theme, cf. Luke 1:51-53). Those who enjoyed the good things of this world will weep in the afterlife whereas those who weep now will rejoice in the afterlife (cf. Luke 6:20-26). There will be a coming judgment.

Paul seems to have had little difficulty in encouraging his community to judge. He is scandalized that the Corinthians are celebrating a man living with his stepmother as though they are married. Paul says that such a thing is not found even among the Gentiles. He decries their attitude and wonders if they had not read his earlier letter wherein he warned them not to associate with immoral people. For Paul, the community was to be holy, i.e, living in right relationship with God and with others. Those Christians who were boldly living immoral lives were to be excluded (1 Cor 5:1-13).

Yet, this advice from Paul needs to be balanced with gospel stories of forgiveness and reconciliation. Perhaps the most famous is that of the woman caught in adultery.

> *Then the scribes and the Pharisees brought a woman who had been caught in adultery and made her stand in the middle. They said to him, "Teacher, this woman was caught in the very act of committing adultery. Now in the law, Moses commanded us to stone such women. So what do you say?" They said this to test him, so that they could have some charge to bring against him. Jesus bent down and began to write on the ground with his finger. But when they continued asking him, he straightened up and said to them, "Let the one among you who is without sin be the first to throw a stone at her." Again he bent down and wrote on the ground. And in response, they went away one by one, beginning with the elders. So he was left alone with the woman before him. Then Jesus straightened up and said to her, "Woman, where are they? Has no one condemned you?" She replied, "No one, sir." Then Jesus said, "Neither do I condemn you. Go, (and) from now on do not sin any more." (John 8:3-11).*

Balancing the desire to lead a holy life not influenced by negative examples with the command to forgive and reconcile is worked out by each Christian in daily life.

Thus the creed concludes the articles about Jesus. The articles began with Jesus being called Christ. The articles about Jesus mention the incarnation, neglect the public ministry, mention the passion death, resurrection, ascension, neglect the miracles Jesus performed, but mention his future coming as judge. Half of the articles of the creed deal directly with Jesus and nowhere do we read about his presence in the Eucharist, or other sacraments, or the liturgical life of the church. We do not have any ethical directives or commands.

There will be a final judgment of all humanity. Death will not preclude one from being judged. Christ himself will be judge when he comes again.

Summary

DISCUSSION QUESTIONS
cf. CCC §668-682

1. How am I called to act in light of the parables Jesus teaches about judgment?
2. How comfortable am I with a judging Jesus?
3. If I were to be judged now, how would I fare?
4. How do we square the judgment of Jesus with the claim that God wants to save all?

Article 8.   I believe in the Holy Spirit,

Catholics begin each Mass by making the sign of the cross in the name of the Father and of the Son and of the Holy Spirit. The third person of the trinity is the object of belief in the eighth article of the creed, which begins with "I believe in." The Holy Spirit is understood by Christians to be the creative presence of God in the world. It might surprise some to find that the spirit of God, even the Holy Spirit is mentioned in the Old Testament, where it often refers to the dynamic, creative presence of God in the community, In the world, or in an individual.

Old Testament

In the Hebrew Old Testament, the word most often translated as spirit is *rûāh*, whose basic meaning is "wind," or "breath." The term can also refer to the inner disposition and volition of a human being. One's *rûāh* is able to be moved by God.

When *rûāh* is used of God it means the creative, life-giving, prophetic, energizing power of God in the life of the individual and the community.[46] When *rûāh YHWH*[47] or *rûāh elohim*[48] occurs, the meaning is generally "spirit" in the sense that the concepts "wind" and "breath" have been overshadowed, and something even more intangible is meant (e.g., Ps 139:7 cited above). Furthermore, *rûāh YHWH* is associated with the early leadership of Israel by Yahweh that includes deliverance from Egypt, various military actions, prophetic leadership through individuals,[49] and ecstatic prophecy.[50] In biblical literature of a later period, *rûāh* no longer specifies a particular divine act; but rather, it simply refers to "God." Additionally, the noun *qodesh* (holy) is sometimes applied to it. For example, "But they rebelled, and grieved his holy spirit; So he turned on them like an enemy, and fought against them. Then they remembered the days of old and Moses, his servant; Where is he who brought up out of the sea the shepherd of his flock? Where is he who put his holy spirit in their midst;" (Isa 63:10-11). Or again, "Do not drive me from your presence, nor take from me your holy spirit." (Ps 51:13).

New Testament

In that sense the Holy Spirit is not a new concept in the New Testament. Instead, the first Christians used the terminology and names for God's presence as they had to reflect their belief. How was Jesus raised? By the power of the Holy Spirit. ("The spirit of him who raised Jesus from the dead)… That is, Jesus was raised by the dynamic, powerful, creative presence of God. How was Jesus conceived? By the power of the Holy Spirit. "The power of the most high will overshadow you." the Holy Spirit will come upon you. That is, Jesus is conceived by the dynamic, powerful, creative presence of God.

Spirit in Paul's Letters

Paul also contributes much to the Christian understanding of Holy Spirit. Paul, writing in Greek, uses the term *pneuma* (spirit) 120 times[51] and *psychē* (soul) 11 times.[52] These numbers alone indicate that "soul" is not a primary element of discussion for Paul. Rather, he writes about "spirit." The debates in classical Greek literature over the nature of the human soul (*psychē*) are absent from Paul. Rather than engage the philosophers of classical Greece, Paul engages the world around him wearing Old Testament lenses ground by his experience of the resurrected Christ. Paul uses the term both anthropologically and theologically. Anthropologically, Paul usually means by *pneuma* "that aspect of a human being which is the knowing and willing self. As such, it expresses what is especially apt to receive the Spirit of God ([Romans] 1:9; 8:16)."[53] Theologically, rather than non-Christian Greek usage, which uses spirit to speak of ecstatic and rapturous powers, Paul reflects much of the Old Testament concept of "Spirit of God." Thus, he reflects the Old Testament concept of *rûāh*. But for Paul, God's creative, life-giving, prophetic, energizing power in the life of an individual and the community is brought to the Christian by Jesus Christ: "the Lord is the Spirit" (2 Cor 3:17).[54]

Paul never says that Christ is the "Spirit of God" Even so, in Rom 8:9-11 he uses interchangeably the terms "Spirit of God," "the Spirit of Christ," "Christ," "the Spirit of him who raised Jesus from the dead," and "his Spirit." Some scholars see triadic language in 1 Cor 12:4-6:

There are different kinds of spiritual gifts but the same Spirit;

there are different forms of service but the same Lord;

there are different workings but the same God who produces all of them in everyone.

In this case, Paul would be using Lord to refer to Jesus. The question is whether Spirit, Lord, and God are three ways of referring to God, or some other meaning that Paul intends. A better example of Paul clearly distinguishing a triad is in 2 Cor 13:13 which we echo in the liturgy: "The grace of the Lord Jesus Christ and the love of God and the fellowship of the holy Spirit be with all of you." Paul's theology, specifically the relationship between God, Jesus, and the Holy Spirit, is not precise. Instead, Paul's theology is functional. He is interested in what Christ has done for the salvation of human beings, and how human beings respond to that gift.

The Spirit itself intercedes for Christians (Rom 8:26); it is the source of their adoption by God (Rom 8:15) and their freedom (2 Cor 3:17).

For Paul the Spirit of God is not an odd power which works magically; the Spirit reveals to the believer God's saving work in Christ and makes possible his understanding and responsible acceptance thereof....

> *For this reason the pneuma, though always God's Spirit and never evaporating into the pneuma given individually to man, is also the innermost ego of the one who no longer lives by his own being but by God's being for him.*[55]

In 1 Cor 2:11-13, Paul compares and contrasts the Spirit of God in a variety of ways:

> *Among human beings, who knows what pertains to a person except the spirit of the person that is within? Similarly, no one knows what pertains to God except the Spirit of God. We have not received the spirit of the world but the Spirit that is from God, so that we may understand the things freely given us by God. And we speak about them not with words taught by human wisdom, but with words taught by the Spirit, describing spiritual realities in spiritual terms.*

In 1 Cor 2:11, Paul draws a parallel between the Spirit of God and the human spirit.[56] In the following verse he contrasts, in a way recalling what he said a few verses earlier,[57] the spirit of the world with the Spirit that is from God. The contrast he draws in 1 Cor 2:13 also spells out the difference between human wisdom and the Spirit. Thus, in 1 Cor 2:11-13, Paul uses spirit of the world to mean the wisdom of this age. The wisdom of this age is in marked contrast to the wisdom of God, which Christians know as a result of their having received the Spirit of God. Later in this letter Paul illustrates the union to be had with the Lord in terms of spirit: "But whoever is joined to the Lord becomes one spirit with him." (1 Cor 6:17).

Paul believes that human beings receive gifts from the Spirit of God. One such gift is tongues, or glossolalia. Paul makes clear that God hears the one who speaks in such a way. Indeed, that one speaks, "in the Spirit": "For one who speaks in a tongue does not speak to human beings but to God, for no one listens; he utters mysteries in spirit." (1 Cor 14:2). Moreover, Paul says of glossolalia:

> *(For) if I pray in a tongue, my spirit*[58] *is at prayer but my mind is unproductive.*

> *So what is to be done? I will pray with the spirit, but I*

will also pray with the mind. I will sing praise with the
spirit, but I will also sing praise with the mind.

Otherwise, if you pronounce a blessing (with) the spirit,
how shall one who holds the place of the uninstructed
say the "Amen" to your thanksgiving, since he does not
know what you are saying? (1 Cor 14:14-16).

Paul also uses *pneuma* as juxtaposed to either *sarx* "flesh"
or *sōma* "body" to contrast the human being dominated by
selfish desires (flesh), with the human being open to receiving
the Spirit of God.

...so that the righteous decree of the law might be
fulfilled in us, who live not according to the flesh but
according to the spirit. For those who live according to
the flesh are concerned with the things of the flesh, but
those who live according to the spirit with the things
of the spirit. The concern of the flesh is death, but the
concern of the spirit is life and peace. For the concern
of the flesh is hostility toward God; it does not submit
to the law of God, nor can it; and those who are in the
flesh cannot please God. But you are not in the flesh;
on the contrary, you are in the spirit, if only the Spirit
of God dwells in you. Whoever does not have the
Spirit of Christ does not belong to him... For if you live
according to the flesh, you will die, but if by the spirit
you put to death the deeds of the body, you will live.
(Rom 8:4-9,13).

The requirement of the law is for Paul its goal. The law
imposed itself on humanity, which was flesh, i.e., bound
by its self-interested desires. It did not give humanity the
power to carry out its precepts. In Paul's view, that situation
has changed because of the Christ event. The Spirit gives
Christians the power to live. Those who live according to the
flesh are those whose lives are dominated by self-centered
interests, carnal pursuits, and carnal thoughts.[59] However,
to live according to the Spirit means that *sarx* does not rule
over one, much less dominate one's perspective. Instead
that one is ruled by the Spirit of God. The striving of one led
by *sarx* is death; the striving of one led by the Spirit of God is
life and peace. The one dominated by flesh is hostile to God

and cannot be submissive to God's law. The self-absorbed cannot please God. Paul reminds his Christian readers that they do not share the condition of sinful humanity, they are not self-absorbed. God's Spirit dwells in them. By that Spirit, Christians can put to death selfish and carnal inclinations and instead truly live.

In his letter to the Galatians, Paul juxtaposes flesh and Spirit in two ways. Paul shows that trusting in circumcision, or works of the flesh, does not offer salvation. Instead, salvation comes about by faith: "But just as then the child of the flesh persecuted the child of the spirit, it is the same now" (Gal 4:29). Paul refers here to Abraham's two sons.[60] Those born according to the flesh (as Ishmael, so the Jews) persecute those born according to the Spirit (as Isaac, so the "Christians"). The distinction is between those who now place their hope in the flesh (circumcision) and those who place their faith in the promised Spirit (Gal 4:23).

Though both passages illustrate a theological meaning, the use of flesh and Spirit in Galatians 4 is slightly different from that expressed in Gal 5:16-17: "I say, then: live by the Spirit and you will certainly not gratify the desire of the flesh. For the flesh has desires against the Spirit, and the Spirit against the flesh; these are opposed to each other, so that you may not do what you want." In chap. 4 Paul shows that God's plan of salvation is by faith rather than by the law. In chap. 5 Paul contrasts two ways of living, but both passages have a theological meaning.

Paul continues the theological distinction of these terms in Galatians 6: "because the one who sows for his flesh will reap corruption from the flesh, but the one who sows for the spirit will reap eternal life from the spirit." (Gal 6:8). The gist of this verse is essentially that of Rom 8:4-9,13, even to the point of similarly balanced phrases.[61] The way of flesh leads to death, but the Spirit leads to eternal life.

Thus, when Paul contrasts flesh and Spirit, he generally means by flesh a human way of life motivated by selfish desires, or earthbound carnal tendencies, while by Spirit he means a human life open to the activity of God's Spirit leading to eternal life.

In sum, Paul uses *pneuma* anthropologically to mean that

aspect of the human being receptive to the influence of God. Theologically his use of *pneuma* is akin to that of the Old Testament, i.e., to express the creative, life-giving power of God at work in an individual or the community. Theologically, Paul contrasts *pneuma* with *sarx* when he wants to indicate humanity cooperating with God as opposed to humanity's pursuit of its own "selfish desires."

Spirit in Mark's Gospel

In Mark, the first gospel to have been composed, we hear the story of Jesus' baptism, "It happened in those days that Jesus came from Nazareth of Galilee and was baptized in the Jordan by John. On coming up out of the water he saw the heavens being torn open and the Spirit, like a dove, descending upon him." (Mark 1:9-10). Note that the text does not say that the Spirit was a dove; but rather, the Spirit descended like a dove. Moreover, Jesus himself saw this.

The identification of the Spirit descending like a dove finds no parallel in the Old Testament. Some will propose a symbolic meaning of a new creation, and find a parallel in Gen 1:2 where the spirit of God hovers over the waters (but there is no mention of dove). Others will propose a symbolic meaning of deliverance, redemption, or peace, and find a parallel in Gen 8:8 where Noah releases a dove (but in Gen 8:8 there is no mention of Spirit). Ultimately, Mark is saying that the ministry of Jesus is inaugurated by the outpouring of the Spirit on him (much like figures in the Old Testament).

Spirit in Luke's Gospel

Luke, who used the gospel of Mark as a source, has shaped the story differently.

> After all the people had been baptized and Jesus also had been baptized and was praying, heaven was opened and the holy Spirit descended upon him in bodily form like a dove. And a voice came from heaven, "You are my beloved Son; with you I am well pleased." (Luke 3:21-22).

Luke makes clear that many people were being baptized, and that Jesus was one of the many. Moreover, the verb is in the perfect tense of the passive voice: "when Jesus also had been baptized." Luke also adds the note about Jesus praying (a favorite Lucan theme). He adds two adjectives: "Holy" to Spirit, again reflecting his interests, and, *sōmatikō(i)* "in bodily form," which occurs only here in the entire New Testament. The latter adjective is used by Luke most likely to show the reality of the event. Luke will do something similar in the resurrection appearance narrative when the risen Lord says, "Look at my hands and my feet, that it is I myself. Touch me and see, because a ghost does not have flesh and bones as you can see I have." (Luke 24:39).

God's spirit is a primary Lucan theme, or better, a character in the two-volume story, who is ever at work in the entire narrative. The Spirit is at work in the prophets. It is by God's spirit that Mary conceives. Jesus is baptized and thus receives the spirit. The spirit empowers Jesus' own ministry. The spirit is a gift of God given not only to Jesus but also at Pentecost to the assembled believers. Thus the spirit guides the early church through its initial difficulties including the decision to lay hands on seven men to assist with the daily distribution. Also, the spirit is given freely by God to Cornelius and his household to such a degree that Peter considers that he would be fighting God himself if he had withheld baptism. So, the spirit is ultimately guiding the entire narrative, from the conception of Jesus, through the ministry of Jesus, to the outpouring of the spirit at Pentecost, including the decision to accept Gentiles without circumcision.

Spirit in Matthew's Gospel

The spirit of God is also prominent in the Gospel of Matthew, who gives us the story of the Great Commission, with its famous triadic text:

> "Go, therefore, and make disciples of all nations, baptizing them in the name of the Father, and of the Son, and of the holy Spirit, teaching them to observe all that I have commanded you. And behold, I am with you always, until the end of the age." (Matt 28:19-20).

In fact, it is from this text that the Church receives the baptismal formula it uses to this very day.

> N., I baptize you in the name of the Father, and of the Son, and of the Holy Spirit.[62]

Spirit in John's Gospel

We would be remiss not to mention the Gospel of John, which conveys a slightly different theology of the Holy Spirit, but one completely congruent of course with the rest of the New Testament. John calls the Spirit the Advocate, or Paraclete. This language conjures up images of a legal assistant, or attorney. In fact, there are four Advocate sayings in the Gospel of John, the first of which occurs in 14:16-17.

And I will ask the Father, and he will give you another Advocate to be with you always, the Spirit of truth, which the world cannot accept, because it neither sees nor knows it. But you know it, because it remains with you, and will be in you.

This is the first of four "advocate" sayings at the Last Supper discourse (the others are 14:25-26; 15:25-26; 16:7-15). The advocate or paraclete is a helper, someone at one's side. We see that from this saying, Jesus was the first advocate. The Father will give them another. The second advocate, the Spirit of truth, has been interpreted as the presence of Jesus after his death and resurrection. Thus, when in the story Jesus promises not to leave them orphans, that he is coming, the evangelist means that Jesus himself is coming to them as the advocate.

In the second advocate saying we have the only time the Paraclete is called "holy spirit." The spirit will teach them all things and remind them of what Jesus himself taught. Thus, the Spirit is related to the earthly Jesus.

The last two advocate sayings come from the redactor (one writing after the initial author). The relationship between Jesus and the Father becomes the model for the relationship between the Spirit and Jesus. Jesus sends the spirit in 15:26-27. In the last advocate saying the Paraclete has a function vis-à-vis the world. The Paraclete convicts (as a prosecuting attorney) the world with respect to three things: sin, righteousness, and judgment. Thus the Paraclete has both an internal and external function. The internal function concerns the life of the church, calling to mind the teachings of Jesus. The external function witnesses to the world and convicts the world.

Thus, clear expressions of a well formulated doctrine of the trinity are basically non existent in the New Testament. Instead we have texts speaking of God in triadic terms (esp. 2 Cor 13:13, Matt 28:19-20). This is not to say that the doctrine of the Trinity is unfounded or has no New Testament support. The roots of the doctrine of the Trinity are certainly found in the New Testament. But theologians wrestled for centuries over how best to speak of the mystery of God, the identity of Jesus, Jesus' relationship to God, the relationship of God's Spirit to Jesus, etc. Even today, many Christians think of the Trinity as two men and a dove (which is not so helpful). It is difficult to express what theologians mean by Trinity in pictures, or in language written at a newspaper level.

Andrei Rublev (1360-1430) was a Russian iconographer whose "Trinity" (or "hospitality of Abraham") has captured the imagination of untold millions. In the icon, Rublev portrays three persons sharing a meal. The scene conjures up thoughts of Gen 18:1-18 in which three angels visit Abraham and Sarah. Yet, in the icon there is no Abraham, no Sarah, only the three visitors. They are portrayed as co-equal, and in communion, or in relationship. This icon then represents for many a different way of imagining trinity.

Balancing a careful articulation of monotheism with three "persons" is difficult. "Person" of course is used in a highly philosophical and technical sense, and not the way we commonly use the term today, to speak of a "center of consciousness," or "freedom." For example, the church uses the term person to distinguish Father, Son, and Spirit. The term nature is used to express the unity of the divine. Thus the three persons of the Trinity share one divine nature. Yet, this language has been problematic and difficult to explain throughout the centuries, not only today. For example, the Koran blasts the notion of three persons in one God.

Koran rails against this idea of a trinity or persons in the one godhead:

O followers of the Book! do not exceed the limits in your religion, and do not speak (lies) against Allah, but (speak) the truth; the Messiah, Isa son of Marium [Jesus son of Mary] is only an apostle of Allah and His Word which He communicated to Marium [Mary] and a spirit from Him; believe therefore in Allah and His apostles, and say not, Three. Desist, it is better for you; Allah is only one God; far be It from His glory that He should have a son, whatever is in the heavens and whatever is in the earth is His, and Allah is sufficient for a Protector [4.171]

Certainly they disbelieve who say: Surely Allah is the third (person) of the three; and there is no god but the one God, and if they desist not from what they say, a painful chastisement shall befall those among them who disbelieve. [5.73] [63]

Certainly Christians today profess belief in the Holy Spirit. Yet, even in this article of the creed, we do not use language saying the "Holy Spirit is God." Instead, the article is introduced by the verb, "I believe" which also introduced the first and second article. In that way, belief in the Father, the Son, and the Holy Spirit are on par with one another. Later councils and later creeds will more fully articulate this belief in the Spirit, adding phrases like, "The Lord, the Giver of Life." So that, in the *Catechism* today § 683-747 more fully explain Catholic belief in the Holy Spirit.

Summary

The Holy Spirit is the creative, dynamic, powerful presence of God in the world, and in the lives of all people. This is the same spirit that hovered over the waters (Gen 1:2), was spoken of in the Psalms (51:13) raised Jesus from the dead (Rom 8:11) and animates the lives of Christians through the centuries, down to this very day. The Spirit is life-giving.

DISCUSSION QUESTIONS
cf. CCC §683-747

1. How meaningful is the Holy Spirit in my own life?
2. How is God the Holy Spirit distinct from God the Father, or God the Son, Jesus Christ?
3. How have I experienced the power of the Holy Spirit in my life?

Article 9.   The holy catholic Church, the communion of saints

The ninth article moves away from the persons of the Trinity and toward the community of believers: the holy catholic church, the communion of saints. The articles concerning the person of the godhead each began with "I believe in…" With the ninth article, there is no preposition "in". We do not believe in the church, we believe the church, and what the church professes in faith. In like manner, we do not believe in resurrection, but we believe that there will be a resurrection. The creed retains the preposition "in" for the persons of the godhead, I believe in the Father… I believe in the Son…I believe in the Holy Spirit.

Holy

To be holy has in some ways a pejorative sense in our culture. To call someone "holy" is not always a compliment. Think of "holy roller," or "holier than thou." Not many people strive to be called holy, even if they strive for holiness in their daily life. But all too often saccharin piety is deemed holy.

The term holy, *sanctus* in Latin, *hagios* in Greek, and *qadosh* in Hebrew has as its root sense "to be set apart." When used of persons, places, or things (and not God) the sense is that the person, place, or thing has been set apart for service to God.

When "holy" is used of God it ultimately refers to his

otherness. The most famous example is found in the prophet Hosea, "For I am God and not man, the Holy One present among you;" (11:9b). Besides God, many other things were considered holy, including for example the land (Amos 7:17; Hos 9:3; Ezek 4:12; to which even today we refer to as the "Holy Land"); priests (1 Chr 23:13; 2 Chr 23:6), vestments (Exod 31:10); water; (Num 5:17), oil (Num 35:25), and time (e.g., a day [Neh 8:9] or a Sabbath [Exod 20:11]). There are many such examples. Especially pertinent for our discussion is the fact that the people of God were considered holy, "you shall be my special possession, dearer to me than all other people, though all the earth is mine. You shall be to me a kingdom of priests, a holy nation." (Exod 19:5b-6a). Thus, the Old Testament concept of God clearly conveys that God is "other than" humanity, "other than" creation. God is set apart, yet intimately near ("among you" Hos 9:11). Persons, places or things can be set apart for service to God as well. Indeed the entire people of God is set apart for him, as a treasured possession.

As we come to the New Testament, we might be surprised to find that holiness is not often mentioned of God. In fact, only a few times is Jesus even called holy (Mark 1:24; Luke 1:35; 4:34; John 6:69; Acts 3:14; 4:27, 30; Rev 3:7). Instead, the term holy is used most often to refer to the Christian people (e.g., Acts 9:13; Phil 4:22a), that is, the church (1 Cor 1:2; 2 Cor 1:1).[64] In fact, 1 Pet 2:9 quotes Exod 19:6 (cited above) in what is believed to be a baptismal homily to Gentile converts.

> But you are "a chosen race, a royal priesthood, a holy nation, a people of his own, so that you may announce the praises" of him who called you out of darkness into his wonderful light. Once you were "no people" but now you are God's people; you "had not received mercy" but now you have received mercy. (1 Pet 2:9-10).

In this way a holy church, a holy people, is that which is set apart from the world for God. The Vatican Document *Lumen Gentium* (§ 9) quotes this same passage from 1 Peter in talking about the Church. The early Christians were to be salt for the earth, the light of the world, a city set on a hill

(Matt 5:13-14). Thus *Lumen Gentium* speaks of the church's role in the world.

> ...*all the faithful of Christ of whatever rank or status,*
> *are called to the fullness of the Christian life and to*
> *the perfection of charity;(4*) by this holiness as such*
> *a more human manner of living is promoted in this*
> *earthly society.... Furthermore, married couples and*
> *Christian parents should follow their own proper path*
> *(to holiness) by faithful love. ... In this manner, they*
> *offer all men the example of unwearying and generous*
> *love; in this way they build up the brotherhood of*
> *charity; in so doing, they stand as the witnesses and*
> *cooperators in the fruitfulness of Holy Mother Church;*
> *by such lives, they are a sign and a participation in*
> *that very love, with which Christ loved His Bride and*
> *for which He delivered Himself up for her.(11*) A*
> *like example, but one given in a different way, is that*
> *offered by widows and single people, who are able to*
> *make great contributions toward holiness and apostolic*
> *endeavor in the Church. Finally, those who engage*
> *in labor-and frequently it is of a heavy nature- should*
> *better themselves by their human labors. They should*
> *be of aid to their fellow citizens. They should raise all*
> *of society, and even creation itself, to a better mode*
> *of existence. Indeed, they should imitate by their lively*
> *charity, in their joyous hope and by their voluntary*
> *sharing of each others' burdens, the very Christ who*
> *plied His hands with carpenter's tools and Who in*
> *union with His Father, is continually working for the*
> *salvation of all men. In this, then, their daily work they*
> *should climb to the heights of holiness and apostolic*
> *activity.*[65]

Thus, Christians today, especially Catholics, are still called to be salt for the earth, to raise all of society to a better mode of existence. It is not enough, in fact, it is inadequate simply or merely to critique the world. Christians are called to transform it by our thoughts and actions, to build a more just society. Perhaps Paul VI said it most succinctly, "if you want peace, work for justice."

Catholic

When the Apostles' Creed mentions the catholic Church, it means not so much the Roman Catholic Church but the universal church. The term *katholikos* in Greek simply means "universal." The Christians in the early church realized that their local church was part of something bigger, more universal. These churches did not exist in isolation but held common beliefs and practices that united them as one universal (catholic) church.

Even so, the term "catholic" when used in this article has been understood by many to be the Roman Catholic Church. For example, this is the one word that Martin Luther changed in the Apostles' Creed. In fact, he changed this word to "Christian" so that in his Apostles' Creed the phrase read, "the holy Christian church, the communion of saints."[66]

Church

The word church in Greek is *ekklēsia* which means an "assembly," or those "called out" (from the Greek *ek* [out] + *kaleō* [call or choose]). Though there is a universal sense to the church, as we saw above, there is also particularity.

For example, though Paul can speak of the churches of God in Judea (1 Thess 2:15; Gal 1:22), he also speaks of the church of God in Corinth (1 Cor 1:2; 2 Cor 2:1). Especially in 1 Cor, the sense of unity had by partaking of the one cup and one bread is more than that of an individual church.

> *The cup of blessing that we bless, is it not a participation in the blood of Christ? The bread that we break, is it not a participation in the body of Christ? Because the loaf of bread is one, we, though many, are one body, for we all partake of the one loaf. (1 Cor 10:16-17).*

Moreover, Paul concludes chapter 10 of 1 Corinthians with an appeal for them not to give offense to the "church of God" without modifier (in Judea, in Corinth, etc.). Paul claims that "you are the Christ's body" (1 Cor 12:27).

By the time we have Colossians and Ephesians, there has been a development of Pauline ecclesiology. No longer are Christians the body of Christ. Instead, Christ "is the head of the body, the church" (Col 1:18; cf. Eph 5:23). Thus, the Colossian/Ephesian letters develop the ecclesiology we find in Paul. The Christians as it were make up the body, with

Christ as its head. Christ is the principle of unity.

The marks of unity held by the church are outlined in Ephesians 4:4-6:

> *one body and one Spirit, as you were also called to the one hope of your call; one Lord, one faith, one baptism; one God and Father of all, who is over all and through all and in all.*

If we arrange these marks of unity by bullet point, we can more clearly see that there are seven:

1. One Body
2. One Spirit
3. One Hope
4. One Lord
5. One Faith
6. One Baptism
7. One God and Father of all, who is over all and through all and in all.

Intriguingly, "One Church" is not enumerated. The ecclesiological terminology is instead "one body." This scripture passage has ramifications on ecumenical relations. Today when a non-Catholic baptized Christian enters the Catholic church, there is no need to "re-baptize." The Catholic church recognizes the baptism of other Christian traditions (Episcopalians, Methodists, Lutherans, etc.). In this way we are true to the ideal expressed in Eph 4:4-6; there is one baptism.

Vatican II in its document *Lumen Gentium* (§8) said that the Church of Christ "subsists in" the Catholic Church. This was a deepening and development of the doctrine of the church. The document did not use the word "is" but preferred "subsists in" to bring out "more clearly the fact that there are 'numerous elements of sanctification and of truth' which are found outside her structure, but which 'as gifts properly belonging to the Church of Christ, impel towards Catholic Unity.'"[67]

So we see that the issues involved in ecclesiology as stated in article nine of the Apostles' Creed are still very much alive and current.

Communion of saints

As expressed in this article of the creed, the communion of saints make up the church. When we speak of saints, we mean those canonized by the church, such as Mary, St. Francis of Assisi, St. Catherine of Siena, St. Augustine, as well as the saints who have not been canonized, or officially declared so. For example, Paul addressed many of his letters to the "holy ones" or "saints." Often today saint has a pejorative sense. It is not a compliment to say of someone, "he thinks he's a saint." But in antiquity Paul exhorted his audience by reminding them of who they were, "saints." Thus, they should act like it.

It is said that Dorothy Day did not want to be named a saint, because if she were, she would no longer be perceived as "real." Saints are those whose images we revere in statues (marble or plastic), or on holy cards. Saints are/were real people who became upset, dealt with frustration, faced adversity and opposition, were mothers, fathers, priests, religious, royalty, and paupers. To be a saint is to exemplify the life of Christ in this or that particular time and locale, set of circumstances, and the like. Each of us is called to be a saint in our own way. Being a saint is not relegated to the special few, but is the vocation of each and every person called by Christ in baptism.

It is no accident that the creed refers to the "communion" of saints. Together, the saints who make up the church are themselves a community. This is not rugged individualism, or a go-it-alone approach. For Christians, we are in this together, connected to all those who have come before us, and all those who will come after us, but perhaps most importantly, all those who are with us now. Christians are to respect the common good, and work with each other in mind. Together, we are a community.

Summary

Those who profess this creed form a community of faith, a communion of saints. Together they are an assembly, an *ekklēsia*, a church that both universal and particular. The community of believers is set apart from the world for service to God and one another in the world.

DISCUSSION QUESTIONS
cf. CCC §748-975

1. In what ways does Eucharist engender unity in the church today?
2. Who is my favorite saint? Why?
3. What would ecumenical relations look like if we focused on the seven principles of unity found in Eph 4:4-6?

Article 10.   The forgiveness of sins,

Though "forgiveness of sins" is a hallmark of Christianity, its roots are in the Old Testament (Exod 32:32; Lev 4:20; 5:6), where the term "sin" is often used in the sense of a debt or guilt for having committed an offense. Thus, God's forgiveness of sin is the release of the perpetrator from the guilt and debt incurred by the offense.

Old Testament

In the example from Exodus cited above, Moses intercedes before God on behalf of the people, who had fashioned the golden calf at Aaron's instigation. Moses implores God, "If you would only forgive their sin!" (Exod 32:32). In that story the Lord does not in fact forgive their sin, but punishes only those who did sin. (This is actually seen as a good thing in that the people are not punished collectively, only individually, based on their actions.)

In the book of Leviticus forgiveness of sin most often comes about by ritual action performed by the levitical priests. Sins were seen as incurring debt against God. Atonement could be made by sacrifice, based on the sin that was committed. Certain sins required more than others. For example, a sin of the community required the sacrifice of a bullock (Lev 4:13-21) whereas the sin of an individual person (not a priest or prince) required a she-goat or a lamb

(Lev 4:27-35). Ritual impurity also required sin offering and holocaust for atonement (e.g., Lev 14:19-20).

The Day of Atonement was an annual day of fast and self-denial by which all Israel was cleansed of sin (Lev 16; esp. 16:30). The ritual involved a blood sacrifice in the sanctuary, and the sending away of the scapegoat, thereby sending away the sins of the people (Lev 16:20-22).

New Testament

These Old Testament images of atonement being made for sins provided fertile ground for the imagination of early Christian thinkers. For example, the Letter to the Hebrews casts the salvific work of Jesus in terms of a heavenly Day of Atonement ceremony (Heb 6-9), with Jesus himself as high priest, offering his own blood.

Paul, in the letter to the Romans, talks about Jesus being the new means of expiation (Rom 3:25) vis-à-vis the Day of Atonement ritual. In Col 1:14 and Eph 1:7 the author speaks of forgiveness of transgressions. Otherwise, nowhere else in the Pauline corpus do we find the phrase "forgiveness of sins."

Christianity is known for teaching forgiveness of sin. The phrase, "forgiveness of sins" or related variants occur throughout the New Testament, most especially in the Gospel of Luke and in Acts.[68] Of course, the term "forgiveness," or "forgive" also occurs quite often in the New Testament without modification. John the Baptist preaches a baptism of repentance for the forgiveness of sins (Luke 3:3). Jesus forgives sins (Luke 5:20), In Luke we hear the story of Jesus' words from the cross, "Father, forgive them, they know not what they do." (Luke 23:34). The Risen Lord commissions the disciples to forgive sins (Luke 24:47). The Lucan theme of forgiveness extends throughout the gospel and into the Acts of the Apostles (2:38; 5:31; 10:43; 13:38; 26:18).

We probably think we instinctively know what forgiveness of sins mean. But, what does Luke mean by the term? The Greek term Luke uses for forgiveness is *aphesis*, which in layman's speech of the day most often was used in terms of cancellation of debt. Therefore, the expression "the power to forgive sin" refers to the power to release human beings from their debts (sins) before God.

This call for God to forgive sins is seen also in the Lord's Prayer, preserved for us both in Matthew and in Luke. Though it is Matthew's version of the prayer that Christians have memorized for centuries, it is worthwhile to compare the two versions.

Matthew	Luke
Our Father in heaven, hallowed be your name, your kingdom come, your will be done, on earth as in heaven. Give us today our daily bread; and forgive us our debts, as we forgive our debtors; and do not subject us to the final test, but deliver us from the evil one. *Matt 6:9b-13*	Father, hallowed be your name, your kingdom come. Give us each day our daily bread and forgive us our sins for we ourselves forgive everyone in debt to us, and do not subject us to the final test. *Luke 11:2b-4*

The Catholic Biblical Scholar, John P. Meier, has an excellent discussion of the Our Father and its historicity in volume two of *A Marginal Jew*.[69] In that book, Meier analyzes the differences between the Matthean and Lukan versions of the prayer to find that Matthew's version of the prayer has been influence by a liturgical setting (note the several additions) and Luke's version has been influence by a shift away from a future eschatology toward more present day concerns (see the first two "we petitions").

By carefully discerning what Matthew and Luke may have each added to the prayer, and then postulating an original, Meier proposes this:

(Address)	Father,

I. "You petitions"

(1. petition)	hallowed be your name.
(2. petition)	Your Kingdom come.

II. "We petitions"

(1. petition)	Our daily bread give us today.
(2. petition)	And forgive us our debts as we forgive our debtors.
(3. petition)	And do not lead us to the test.

and then comments:

The structure is tight and laconic, eminently suitable for memorization. Jeremias discerns in the Aramaic a pattern of a two–and four beat rhythm, along with a number of rhymes. The address to God, made up of a single word, is followed by two short, carefully paralleled petitions focusing directly on "the matters of God" (your name, your kingdom). These in turn are followed by three somewhat longer petitions focusing on the needs of the petitioners (our bread, our debts, do not lead us). One gets the impression of a short prayer that is so direct and to the point that it almost offends the sensibilities of those who are accustomed to the longer rhythmic phrases of the Matthean version. The hypothetical form, while not the prayer of an isolated individual (as the "we" petitions show), has not undergone either the rhetorical expansions fostered by liturgical use within a community (the Matthean form, which phrases parallel to those in Jewish synagogal prayers) or a shift away from a thoroughgoing future-eschatological vision toward the ongoing daily needs of life in the present world (the first and second "we petitions" in Luke). This fits well with the idea that the hypothetical form had its original Sitz im Leben [setting in life] not in the early church but among the disciples of the historical Jesus when they were still a loose band gathered around him. Certainly the very fact that this Aramaic form existed earlier than either of the two forms of the prayer that were already traditional in the churches of Mathew and Luke prior to the composition of their Gospels-indeed probably before the Q tradition was collected–argues for a very early date for the prayer. In Addition, a pointer to a Palestinian-Aramaic milieu can be found in the use of "debt" and "debtor" for "sin" and "sinners".[70]

Thus, Jesus himself most likely taught the early disciples to forgive "debts" as they (we) forgive those in debt to us. Much of the New Testament expects the imminent judgment of God upon the world. God's forgiveness in effect exempts one from that fearful day. In this prayer, Jesus offers us a troubling thought. That is, our forgiveness of others will determine God's forgiveness of us. This concept is difficult for the modern believer who is told often that God forgives all, God reconciles all, God calls all. However, as Jesus would have it, even Christian disciples may not be forgiven if they do forgive others in their own lives.

Immediately following the Lord's Prayer in the Gospel of Matthew, Jesus issues this promise:

> *If you forgive others their transgressions, your heavenly Father will forgive you. But if you do not forgive others, neither will your Father forgive your transgressions. (Matt 6:14-15)*

This somewhat troubling idea is not limited to the Lord's Prayer but finds an echo in many parables. For example, the Gospel of Matthew records the parable of aborted forgiveness in 18:23-35. In that story, a man who owes much to the ruler is forgiven. In fact, the story says he owed ten thousand talents, which in that time was a fantastic amount never to be repaid. In fact, it would be like saying he owed millions and millions of dollars. The point is that he is not able to repay the money. The ruler in his kindness recognizes this and forgives the debt in its entirety. The released man turns around and extracts a pithy amount (a denarius, or the wages earned in one day) from another. When the ruler finds out, he does not mince words, "You worthless wretch!" is his name for the man, who is sent to the torturers until he pays back the entire debt. Jesus concludes by warning his disciples, "So will my heavenly Father do to you, unless each of you forgives his brother from his heart" (Matt 18:35). The man who was initially released from his debt did not reciprocate. We are reminded that God's gracious act of mercy and forgiveness is to be emulated, not hoarded. God's forgiveness can in fact be revoked on the last day.

Other such stories in the New Testament include the story of the final judgment, again in the Gospel of Matthew (25:31-46). For in the Gospel of Matthew, not everyone who cries "Lord, Lord" will be saved, but only those who do the will of the Father (7:21; 12:50). "For as you judge, so will you be judged, and the measure with which you measure will be measured out to you" (Matt 7:2).

Luke of course echoes this thought with a slight variation:

"Stop judging and you will not be judged. Stop condemning and you will not be condemned. Forgive and you will be forgiven. Give and gifts will be given to you; a good measure, packed together, shaken down, and overflowing, will be poured into your lap. For the measure with which you measure will in return be measured out to you." (Luke 6:37-38).

Emulating the forgiveness that has been extended to us is a hallmark of Christianity, and the basis of our salvation.

The gospel of John also has a strong theology of forgiveness of sins. Indeed, in John's story of Jesus' resurrection appearance before his disciples, Jesus tells them: "Receive the holy Spirit. Whose sins you forgive are forgiven them, and whose sins you retain are retained." (John 20:22b-23). Though Jesus has conquered sin, the mission of the disciples is to forgive sins. In a sense, the disciples' vocation is now to forgive sins.

This mission, or calling to forgive sins, finds attestation also in the Letter of James, 5:15-16 wherein the author reminds them, "the prayer of faith will save the sick person, and the Lord will raise him up. If he has committed any sins, he will be forgiven. Therefore, confess your sins to one another and pray for one another, that you may be healed. The fervent prayer of a righteous person is very powerful."

Certainly, the church celebrates the forgiveness of sins in the Sacrament of Reconciliation when the priest says according to the Rite, "God, the Father of mercies, through the death and resurrection of his Son has reconciled the world to himself and sent the Holy Spirit among us for the forgiveness of sins; through the ministry of the Church may God give you pardon and peace, and I absolve you from your sins in the name of the Father, and of the Son, and of the Holy Spirit."

Forgiving sins happens not only in the confessional but each day, as the passage from James would indicate. When we think in terms of our own lives, much healing may happen when we step up to the person we've hurt and say, "I'm sorry. Please forgive me." and then experience the reconciliation that most often follows.

The church also teaches that forgiveness for daily faults (venial/lesser sins) also occurs by reception of the Eucharist.[71]

In the early church, forgiveness of sins was one way of expressing what God had done for humanity in Christ. At times it was said that our debts were forgiven. The language is metaphorical. It is as though humanity because of its sin owed a debt to God that we could not pay. God responded with the Christ, who cancelled the debt, or paid it on our behalf. Some theologians queried to whom the debt was paid, but this is taking the metaphor too far. The point is that sins have been forgiven because of Christ. Now, individual Christians are to continue the effects of this cosmic event by confessing sins to one another, and forgiving one another.

Summary

Forgiving sins is the mission of the church on earth (John 20:23). Christians are to be known for their forgiveness. In the end, our forgiveness of others will be the measure with which we are forgiven.

DISCUSSION QUESTIONS
cf. CCC §976-987

1. When is the last time I truly apologized to someone I hurt, and asked for their forgiveness?
2. Who are those that come to mind when I hear the word, "Saint?" Why do I think of these people? What am I called to do in my own life to be a saint?
3. What will forgiveness look like for me personally if my own measurement of forgiveness is the standard?

Article 11.   the resurrection of the body,

This article of the creed is based on Jesus' being raised, in as much as Christ is the "first fruits of those who have fallen asleep" (1 Cor 15:20). That is, what happened to Christ will happen to us. So when Christians proclaim the resurrection of the body, they are proclaiming belief in their own resurrection from the dead. This belief in resurrection set Christians apart from most other religions in antiquity, yet it was an expression of an Old Testament belief punctuated certainly by the resurrection of Jesus.

We recall that there are Old Testament stories of the dead being raised to life. For example, Elijah raised the widow's son in 1 Kings 17:17-24 and Elisha raised the Shunammite woman's son in 2 Kings 4:8-37. Even in the New Testament there are stories of raising from the dead. Jesus raised Lazarus (John 11:38-44); the widow's son at Nain (Luke 7:11-15) and Jairus' daughter (Matt 9:18-19, 23-25; Mark 5:22-24, 35-43; Luke 8:41-42,49-56). Even Peter and Paul are said to have raised the dead (Acts 9:36-42; 20:7-12).

The belief in the "resurrection of the body" has been a standard of Christian faith for centuries. However, the way this article of faith has been articulated has differed. For example, the Nicene creed proclaims a belief in the resurrection of the dead. This is closer to biblical data for nowhere in the New Testament does the phrase, "resurrection of the body" occur. Instead, the term is often, "resurrection of the dead" (e.g., Matt. 22:31; Luke 20:35; Acts 4:2; 17:32; 23:6; 24:21; 26:23; Rom. 1:4; 1 Cor 15:12,13,21,42; Heb 6:2; 1 Pet 1:3). The Easter proclamation was not, "the body of Jesus has risen!" But "The Lord has truly been raised!" (Luke 24:34).

Resurrection

Resurrection itself is a Semitic concept, springing from an anthropological view of the human being as a unified whole. In Hebrew there is scarcely a word for "body" though there is a term that means "corpse." In the Old Testament the human being is generally portrayed as one thing with different aspects including thoughts, feelings, will, desire, flesh, spirit, heart. Thus, the world view that spoke of resurrection understood it as a restoration of the whole person. It is as though once a person dies, that person is dead. Death is permanent. Resurrection reverses that condition, and the dead person is brought to life in totality.

The anthropological view reflected in Hebrew differed with that of the Greek world, which saw the human being primarily in terms of body and soul. The soul was thought to be immortal, and shed the body at death to live forever. So, once this notion of resurrection of the dead was brought to a Greek view of the person as body and soul, interesting developments occurred.

Paul himself perhaps faced this very issue in Greek-speaking Corinth when he was asked about the resurrection, "with what kind of body will they come back?" (1 Cor 15:35). His answer is "You fool!" (1 Cor 15:36). There must be a transformation, as there is with the seed and the tree. What we sow as a seed is the body. God will raise us to new life in a way that we cannot imagine. This will happen in a blink of an eye. Flesh and blood, the body as it is now, will not inherit the kingdom. Instead, there must be a transformation (1 Cor 15:35-58).

Paul preached the resurrection to his audience, many of whom lived in a world without the hope of life after death (cf. 1 Thess 4:13). Some early Christians (perhaps co-workers of Paul?) proclaimed that the resurrection had already happened, and that Christians already lived a life of resurrection.

Hymenaeus and Philetus… have deviated from the
truth by saying that (the) resurrection has already
taken place and are upsetting the faith of some. (2 Tim
2:17b-18).

Paul is clear in stating that the resurrection will be a future event for those who have died in Christ (1 Thess 4:13-18).

Though Paul witnessed the risen Christ, he never describes the experience, but we find three passages wherein he makes reference to it: (God) "was pleased to reveal his son to me" (Gal 1:15-16), "Have I not seen Jesus our Lord?" (1 Cor 9:1); and "Last of all, as to one born abnormally, he appeared to me." (1 Cor 15:8). None of these examples comes close to Luke's three-fold description of Paul's encounter with the risen Lord on the road to Damascus that we read in Acts (chaps. 9, 22, and 26). In fact, the reader of Paul's letters is left grasping for details of the encounter that Luke depicts so vividly. Paul is content to make reference to his encounter by means of these pithy statements.

Despite Paul's forceful teaching in 1 Cor 15, early Christians such as Justin Martyr (1 Apology 18-19) began to speak of the resurrection *of the body* and the immortality of the soul. No longer was resurrection a restoration of the whole person. Resurrection was now understood to be a raising up of the corpse to be united with the immortal soul. Instead of "body," some theologians preferred the term "flesh" (e.g., Irenaeus, *AH* 5.14.1). Indeed, many early Christian creeds proclaim belief in the resurrection of the flesh. The teaching of the scholastic period about resurrection is summarized in one line of the Second General Council of Lyons (1274), "we believe also in the true resurrection of this flesh that we now bear."[72]

Ultimately, resurrection is a core belief of Christianity. For if Christ has not been raised, our faith is in vain. As St. Paul proclaims,

But if Christ is preached as raised from the dead, how
can some among you say there is no resurrection of
the dead? If there is no resurrection of the dead, then
neither has Christ been raised. And if Christ has not
been raised, then empty (too) is our preaching; empty,

too, your faith. Then we are also false witnesses to God, because we testified against God that he raised Christ, whom he did not raise if in fact the dead are not raised. For if the dead are not raised, neither has Christ been raised, and if Christ has not been raised, your faith is vain; you are still in your sins. (1 Cor 15:12-17).

Thus, if we do not proclaim resurrection, our faith is in vain. In fact, if Christ was not raised from the dead would Christianity have developed? The disciples scattered after the crucifixion, fearing they were to die next! The resurrection of Christ transformed death, and even gave death meaning. "For the wages of sin is death, but the gift of God is eternal life in Christ Jesus our Lord." (Rom 6:23). In the resurrection, Christ conquered death. Now, for Christians there is hope of a future life with Christ, as Paul says in 1 Thess 4:17b "Thus we [the dead and the living] shall always be with the Lord." Since Christ was raised, Christians believe that we too will be raised, for Christ is the first-fruits of those who have died (1 Cor 15:20,23). Christ's resurrection is, as it were, a promise for us. What happened to Christ will happen to those who believe in him. Death is not the final state for the Christian.

Problems with resurrection?

Today, many Christians still have problems with resurrection.[73] We hear questions such as, what age will I be when I am raised? Will I be raised with a thirty-year old body, a fifty-year old body, a seventy-year old body? What if my corpse were cremated? How does the flesh return?

These questions have vexed theologians for centuries. It was Athenagoras who wrote the first Christian treatise specifically on this subject, aptly titled, *De Resurrectione* or "On Resurrection." Since he makes no mention of Christ and does cite the pagan physician Galen, he probably addressed the work to non-Christians. In it he discusses crass, physical problems associated with resurrection. For example, if a human being consumes an animal which itself had consumed a human being, how will God keep the parts straight at the resurrection (*Res.* 4)? His answer basically consisted in the claim that this task would not be difficult for God, the creator of the world (*Res.* 2-3; 9). The resurrected bodies would in fact be made of reconstituted parts from their earthly bodies

(*Res.* 7). This led later theologians to wonder whether God might use one's former arm to make that same one's resurrected leg, or whether a former arm would have to be resurrected as an arm.

When we proclaim a resurrection of the flesh or resurrection of the body the question often comes back to a variation of the famous chain consumption argument that Methodius addressed, or we delve into questions that created theological problems regarding hair, blood, sweat, aborted fetuses, at what age we would appear, whether we would be handsome or ugly, husky or slim, male or female! Ultimately, these are not the questions that contribute to the profundity of the resurrection; rather, they drag it into the mire of the ridiculous, as Jerome himself experienced:

> And to those of us who ask whether the resurrection
> will exhibit from its former condition hair and teeth,
> the chest and the stomach, hands and feet, and other
> joints, then, no longer able to contain themselves and
> their jollity, they burst out laughing and adding insult
> to injury they ask if we shall need barbers, and cakes,
> and doctors, and cobblers, and whether we believe
> that the genitalia of which sex would rise, whether our
> (men's) cheeks would rise rough, while women's would
> be soft and whether the bodies would be differentiated
> based on sex. Because, if we surrender this point, they
> immediately proceed to female genitalia and everything
> else in and around the womb. They deny that singular
> members of the body rise, but the body, which is
> constituted from members, they say rises. [74]

Today we have a better understanding of biology and the created world than they did in antiquity. We know that our bodies regenerate nearly every single cell in seven years or so. I am literally not the same as I was ten years ago! Yet, there is some fundamental identity that stays true. The early Christian thinker Origen put it this way. "River" is an appropriate name for the body.[75] In doing so, he held two opposing concepts together: identity and change. Origen however was condemned for other views, so it was the thinking of Jerome and Augustine, following Athenagoras in accenting the resurrection of this physical body, that would form the bedrock of Scholastic and later theology.

When we ask like the Corinthians "with what sort of body will they come back," (1 Cor 15:35) we can hear Paul's answer still echoing from centuries ago, "You fool!" (1 Cor 15:36). What we sow is a bare kernel. It must be transformed. Flesh and blood shall not inherit the kingdom of God. As Christ is the first fruits of the resurrection, what we say about Christ's resurrection dictates what we say about the general resurrection. Christ is no longer subject to death, for he has been raised to new life, seated at the right hand of God, exalted in glory.

These stories of raising the dead from the Old Testament and the New Testament cited above each ended in death again for those who were raised. That is, Lazarus has not been walking the earth for 2000 years. The widow's son from Nain has not been walking the earth since being raised. Both he and Lazarus ultimately died after being raised. Too often we confuse "resurrection of the body" with a resurrection more akin to that of Lazarus than that of Jesus. We might refer instead to the resuscitation of Lazarus, or the resuscitation of the widow's son from Nain. For in calling these New Testament stories "resuscitation" we are more accurately describing the theological import of the story.

Jesus was not merely resuscitated. Jesus was raised from the dead to new life. His being raised was qualitatively different than the raising/resuscitation of Lazarus, or the raising/resuscitation of the widow's son from Nain. Jesus' resurrection may also be called exaltation, glorification, ascension, and seated at the right of God. In this way, when we claim that God raised Jesus from the dead, we are saying more than God resuscitated the limp crucified corpse of Jesus.

When in the Apostles' Creed we proclaim belief in the resurrection of the body, we are proclaiming that Christ is the first fruits of the resurrection. We will share in the resurrection of Christ with everything it means to be human. We will not be disembodied souls, or revivified corpses, but resurrected human beings, raised to a new and glorious life with God and one another.

There is future hope. Death does not mark an end but a change.[76] I will not be a disembodied spirit but a spiritual body (1 Cor 15:44). There will be a transformation (1 Cor 15:51-54).

Summary

DISCUSSION QUESTIONS
cf. CCC §988-1019

1. What does the *Catechism* say about the resurrection of Christ?
2. What will happen when I am raised from the dead?
3. How do I understand the human person, as a unity of body/soul, or in some other way?
4. How do I experience the power of the paschal mystery in my own life?

Article 12.   and the life everlasting. Amen.

The final statement of the creed concerns the final destiny of believers, eternal life. At the same time it expresses a fundamental hope of humanity, everlasting life. The question that the rich man asks Jesus is perhaps the question asked by each individual human being. It concerns our final destiny, "Good Teacher, what must I do to inherit eternal life?" (Mark 10:17).

The idea of eternal life was expressed by some Greek thinkers using the term immortal soul. Plato for example believed that at death a human being shed the body (the tomb of the soul) and the immortal soul would live forever in the realm of the forms.[77]

Old Testament

The Old Testament too reflects a gradual awakening to the idea of everlasting life. In Genesis for example, Enoch is said not to have died, but to have "walked with God" (Gen 5:21-24). Other individuals are taken up such as Elijah, who "went up to heaven in a whirlwind." (2 Kings 2:11). But despite these few examples, most Old Testament figures simply died in one way or another. Everlasting life was not among the articles of belief for the patriarchs; and, depending on how one defines everlasting life, this belief was non-existent throughout most of Old Testament times.

Some of the early ideas of eternal life were associated with offspring. That is, a person lived through his descendants. This is one reason why it was so important to produce offspring. Other ideas concerning afterlife proposed "*sheol*" or a shadowy, watery underworld one enters at death. The book of Jonah gives us a sense of this place:

> Out of my distress I called to the LORD, and he answered me; From the midst of the nether world [sheol] I cried for help, and you heard my voice. For you cast me into the deep, into the heart of the sea, and the flood enveloped me; All your breakers and your billows passed over me. Then I said, "I am banished from your sight! yet would I again look upon your holy temple." The waters swirled about me, threatening my life; the abyss enveloped me; seaweed clung about my head. Down I went to the roots of the mountains; the bars of the nether world were closing behind me forever, But you brought my life up from the pit, O LORD, my God. (Jonah 2:3-7).

Thus, sheol serves as a poetic image for a pit of despair. Sheol was the realm of the dead, both good and bad. For example, Jacob is said to be in Sheol (Gen 37:35) as well as Dathan and Abiram (Num 16). Sheol was the realm of the graves, the underworld. In this way, the Old Testament shares with the Ancient Near East opinions held about after afterlife. That is, extrabiblical literature from Ugarit, Egypt, or Mesopotamia confirms this sense of Sheol. In one sense, the Old Testament view simply reflects commonly held ideas of the time.

Not until the wisdom literature (about 2nd cent. B.C.) do we see belief in immortality expressed more along the lines of Greek thought, "But the souls of the just are in the hand of God, and no torment shall touch them." (Wis 3:1). Even today, this reading from the book of Wisdom is proclaimed often at Catholic funerals. Thus, at death the soul of a human being is with God.

New Testament

We will not be surprised to see that though the New Testament does not express anthropological views in terms of body and soul, it does express belief in life after death. Christian belief in life after death is informed by the exaltation of Christ. The raising of Christ gives the Christian an insight into life after death. Paul says that Christ is the first fruits of the resurrection (1 Cor 15:20,23). What happened to Christ after death will happen to all those who believe in him. The early Christians, who were for the most part Jews, already had a belief in life after death. Their experience of the risen Christ then added to that belief, or rather informed it.

It is a fundamental Christian belief that life does not end with our time on earth. Instead, we are destined for a life with Christ, with God, as Paul reminds us, "Thus we shall always be with the Lord." (1 Thess 4:17b). This belief is also expressed in parables. For example, at the conclusion of the parable of the final judgment in Matthew, Jesus says, "And these will go off to eternal punishment, but the righteous to eternal life." (Matthew 25:46).

"Eternal life" is also a primary theme in the Gospel of John. In a conversation with Nicodemus Jesus says, "For God so loved the world that he gave his only Son, so that everyone who believes in him might not perish but might have eternal life." (John 3:16). Now this verse has become a popular placard in end zones at football games. Is it so popular because it expresses the kernel of the gospel? If so, this kernel of the gospel does not express resurrection, but rather, eternal life. There is something in the human being that wants to live forever. It is a shared hope, a common dream.

Significant for Catholics is that the Gospel of John later ties eternal life to the Eucharist.

I am the living bread that came down from heaven; whoever eats this bread will live forever; and the bread that I will give is my flesh for the life of the world."

The Jews quarreled among themselves, saying, "How can this man give us (his) flesh to eat?" Jesus said to them, "Amen, amen, I say to you, unless you eat the flesh of the Son of Man and drink his blood, you do not have life within you. Whoever eats my flesh and drinks my blood has eternal life, and I will raise him on the last day. For my flesh is true food, and my blood is true drink. Whoever eats my flesh and drinks my blood remains in me and I in him. Just as the living Father sent me and I have life because of the Father, so also the one who feeds on me will have life because of me. This is the bread that came down from heaven. Unlike your ancestors who ate and still died, whoever eats this bread will live forever." (John 6:51-58).

The Gospel of John indicates clearly that Jesus is the Eternal Word of God made flesh (1:1,14), the incarnate Word of God. (The Latin word "carnis" means "flesh." Think of *carne* at a restaurant. To say "incarnate" is to say "enfleshed"). The unchanging, eternal Word of God descends into the earthly realm and actually changes into, or becomes flesh. The unchanging changes. The eternal becomes temporal. The spiritual becomes carnal. The immaterial becomes material. The Word becomes flesh.

How then does one appropriate to oneself this word become flesh? By listening to the word and consuming the flesh. This is sacramental. Indeed it is an early expression of Catholic sacramentality. Human beings live in the world. God encounters human beings in the world, in all its physical, messy, dirty, changing, temporal ways. For the believer in Jesus, it is not enough to listen to the Word of God. The believer will also literally consume the incarnate Word of God, the enfleshed Word of God.

Early church fathers understood this relationship between eternal life and Eucharist. For example, in his major work, *Against Heresies*, Irenaeus (A.D. 130-202) writes,

> *For just as the bread that is from the earth, when it receives the invocation of God, is no longer common bread, but the Eucharist, consisting of two realities, earthly and heavenly, so also our bodies, receiving the Eucharist, no longer are corruptible, but have the hope of resurrection.* [78]

Thus, the relationship between eternal life and reception of the Eucharist has been a matter of belief since apostolic times.

Eternal life is the promise of God made long ago (Tit 1:2). We find references to it throughout the New Testament in the Gospels, Acts, letters, and even in Jude! (Matt 19:29; Mark 10:30; Luke 18:30; John 3:15,16; 4:14, 36; 5:24; 6:27,40,47,54,68; 10:28; 12:25,50; 17:2,3; Acts 13:46,48; Rom 2:7; 5:21; 6:22,23; Gal 6:8; 1 Tim 1:16; 6:12; Tit 1:2; 3:7; 1 John 1:2; 2:25; 3:15: 5:11,13,20; Jude 1:21). The concept of eternal life is one that is more easily grasped than resurrection of the flesh, or resurrection of the body. Life eternal is, as we have said, a shared hope for humanity.

As a matter of fact, this twelfth article of the creed has seemed so innocuous that it has engendered little debate over the centuries, unlike the previous article on resurrection that had to be clarified by later councils. The same Council of Lyons (1274) cited above as reflecting the summary of Scholastic thought professes this about life everlasting in the same sentence as that of resurrection. So it reads, "we believe also in the true resurrection of this flesh that we now bear, and eternal life."[79] Indeed, the final article of the creed is expressed in only these two words: eternal life.

So, this article has generated little controversy through the centuries. Perhaps this is so precisely because it expresses a common hope shared by humanity. There seems to be something in the human condition that longs for eternal life. The Vatican II document *Gaudium et Spes* (§18) states as much in its section on the Mystery of Death:

> It is in the face of death that the riddle of human existence grows most acute. Not only is man tormented by pain and by the advancing deterioration of his body, but even more so by a dread of perpetual extinction. He rightly follows the intuition of his heart when he abhors and repudiates the utter ruin and total disappearance of his own person. He rebels against death because he bears in himself an eternal seed which cannot be reduced to sheer matter. All the endeavors of technology, though useful in the extreme, cannot calm his anxiety; for prolongation of biological life is unable to satisfy that desire for higher life which is inescapably lodged in his breast.[80]

For Christians, belief in eternal life is an article of faith. Ultimately, life has meaning and we are destined for eternity.

That message needs to be proclaimed today as ever before, when we face a "dictatorship of relativism" which seeks to strip ultimate meaning for human existence. Today, like the days when St. Paul wrote to the Thessalonians, Christians are not to be like the rest who have no hope. It is this hope of being forever with the Lord that drives our baptismal call to proclaim the good news to those who are far off, and to those who are near. The Lord has risen. Our destiny awaits!

Summary

Though this life on earth will end, the life to come with Christ will never end. "Eye has not seen, ear has not heard, nor has it even entered the human heart, what God has ready for those who love him" (1 Cor 2:9).

DISCUSSION QUESTIONS
cf. CCC §1020-1060

1. What is the relationship between Eternal Life and Eucharist?
2. What do we believe happens at death?

Conclusion

Today, when the Apostles' Creed is heard primarily at children's liturgies, or at the praying of the Rosary, it is good to step back and study this ancient articulation of the faith. Though we recognize that each apostle did not contribute one article, we see that in many respects the beliefs that the creed professes are foreshadowed in the Old Testament, found expressed in the New Testament, and are thus apostolic. It helps our understanding to examine what the authors of the New Testament meant, as well as what the early church meant when they expressed faith. In so doing, we might come to a deeper understanding of our own faith.

The articles of the creed are perhaps more germane today than ever. Yet, we understand that the entirety of our faith is not encapsulated in the creed. For, there is no mention of Sacraments, not even Eucharist. There is no mention of Liturgy, or communal prayer, or the Our Father. Still, the creed has a unique position in the life of the church. It reminds us of core beliefs, some stated in metaphorical images and certain "obvious" statements, which can sometimes be forgotten.

In looking to refresh our knowledge of the faith, there is perhaps no better starting point than the Apostles' Creed.[81]

1 This legend has its roots in Sermon 240 of Augustine, which is now considered to have been written in the 9th century A.D. and falsely attributed to Augustine (Kelly, *ECC*, 3).

2 Ignatius, *Trallians*, 9. taken from: http://www.ccel.org/ccel/schaff/anf01. v.iv.ix.html

3 Hippolytus, *Apostolic Tradition* 21.9-18; http://www.bombaxo.com/ hippolytus.html

4 unum Deum Dominum nouit, creatorem uniuersitatis, et Christum Iesum ex uirgine Maria filium Dei creatoris, et carnis resurrectionem, legem et prophetas cum euangelicis et apostolicis litteris miscet…,(*De praescriptione* 36 [CCSL 1.217]).

5 Regula quidem fidei una omnino est, sola immobilis et irreformabilis, credendi scilicet in unicum Deum omnipotentem, mundi conditorem, et filium eius Iesum Christum, natum ex uirgine Maria, crucifixum sub Pontio Pilato, tertia die resuscitatum a mortuis, receptum in caelis, sedentem nunc ad dexteram Patris, uenturum iudicare uiuos et mortuos per carnis etiam resurrectionem. (*De virginibus velandis* 1.3 [CCSL 2.1209]):

6 J. N. D. Kelly. *Rufinus: A Commentary on the Apostles' Creed*. ACW 20: Newman: New York, NY; 1978, 15-16

7 I am following here the first chapter of ECC. The reader is directed to that study to find a more thorough treatment of the subject matter.

8 St. Ambrose, Ep. 42.5 (PL 16.1125b).

9 Scholars judge Sermon 240 of De Symbolo to be a late, spurious work (cf. footnote 1).

10 SERMO CCXL. De Symbolo IV.

Quid quisque apostolus de Symbolo composuit. [Col.2189] Remissiones peccatorum septem. Decimo die post ascensionem, discipulis prae timore Judaeorum congregatis, Dominus promissum Paracletum misit; quo veniente ut candens ferrum inflammati, omniumque linguarum peritia repleti, Symbolum composuerunt. Petrus dixit, Credo in Deum Patrem omnipotentem. Ubi dicit Patrem, intelligitur Filius, intelligitur et Spiritus: utriusque etenim harum trium personarum substantia inseparabilis. Omnipotentem dicit, quia cum ei nihil sit impossibile, malum non potest; quia si posset, omnipotens non esset. Creatorem coeli et terrae: per Patrem omnia significat. Andreas dixit, Et in Jesum Christum Filium ejus. Jesus nomen proprium interpretatur Salvator; Christus appellativum, hebraice dicitur Unctus; ungi enim Prophetae et reges solebant. Unicum Dominum nostrum. Unicum dicit secundum naturam: Adam et Eva etiam Dei filii sunt, sed adoptivi. Jacobus dixit, Qui conceptus est de Spiritu sancto: non quod Spiritus pater ejus fuerit; sed quod per administrationem Spiritus sancti, et eo cooperante in fide Mariae conceptus est. Natus ex Maria virgine; quae virgo concepit, et virgo peperit, virgoque permansit. Joannes dixit, Passus sub Pontio Pilato: hoc dicit, ne in alium Christum credamus, nisi in illum, qui in tempore Pilati passus est; nam multi, sicut ait, antichristi falso dicent, Ego sum Christus **(Matth. XXIV, 24)**. Crucifixus, mortuus, et sepultus, secundum carnem: ad hoc natus est ut crucifigeretur, ad hoc crucifixus ut moreretur, ad hoc mortuus ut resurgeret, ad hoc resurrexit ut nos justificaret. Thomas dixit, Descendit ad inferna: id est, in anima comitante divinitatem, corpore vero in sepulcro quiescente. Tertia die resurrexit a mortuis; ut nobis exemplum et fidem resurrectionis ostenderet. Jacobus dixit, Ascendit ad coelos: in ipsa carne, in qua natus est et passus, in ipsa resurrexit et victor coelos ascendit. Sedet ad dexteram Dei Patris omnipotentis. Dextera Patris prosperitatem vitae nostrae; sinistra autem significat poenam inferni. Philippus dixit, Inde venturus est judicare vivos et mortuos: in quo ascendit corpore, venturus est ad judicium, justos a peccatoribus separabit. Bartholomaeus dixit, Credo in Spiritum sanctum, a quo Pater et Filius in suo opere, vel in catholica fide separari nullo modo possunt. Matthaeus dixit, Sanctam Ecclesiam catholicam: catholicam, id est, universalem, in qua tantum peccata remittuntur, quae omnium haereticorum pravitate repulsa, ab ortu solis usque ad occasum diffunditur. Sanctorum communionem: quia dona sancti Spiritus licet in hac vita diversa sint in singulis, in aeternitate tamen erunt communia in universis; ut quod quisque sanctorum minus habuit in se, hoc in aliena virtute participet. Simon dixit, Remissionem peccatorum. Septem sunt remissiones peccatorum: prima Baptismi, secunda poenitentiae, tertia divinae pietatis, quarta venia per indulgentiam inimicorum, quinta per veram charitatem, sexta per eleemosynam, septima per praedicationem qua errantes convertuntur. Thaddaeus dixit, Carnis resurrectionem: id est, in ipsa carne in qua vivimus, resurgemus; non sexum, sed fragilitatem mutantes. Tunc sancti qui nunc habent singulas stolas, id est, praemium vitae, tunc binas accipient, id est, corporis et animae pretium; peccatores vero duplicem poenam accipient, ut quae in hac vita corpus simul et anima promeruerunt, pariter in illa percipiant. Matthias dixit, Vitam aeternam; quam nullus finis terminabit, nullum vitium foedabit, aegritudo nulla contristabit.

11   Cf. Martin Luther's *Smaller Catechism*, *Larger Catechism*, and various sermons, e.g, *LW* 51.166.

12   E.g., Elizabeth Johnson, *She Who Is (Tenth Anniversary Edition)*. New York: Herder & Herder, 2002. Catherine M. Lacugna, *Freeing Theology: The Essentials of Theology in Feminist Perspective*. New York: HarperOne, 1993.

13   CCC §239.

14   Fitzmyer, *Romans* (AB 33; New York: Doubleday, 1993) 111; J.P.Meier, *A Marginal Jew* vol. 1 (New York: Doubleday, 1991) 205-208.

15   Many times people ask, why don't we call Jesus "Josh" or "Joshua"? The Latin translation of the Greek name is Iesus. In the late middle ages, the consonantal "i" (that is, when "i" precedes a consonant and is pronounced like a "y") became rendered with the "j" sound. Thus, we say "Jesus" even though a direct translation of the name from Hebrew could and would yield "Josh."

16   The term messiah has a "rubber band extension" quality to it, to borrow J. A. Fitzmyer's term ("Qumran Messianism," in *The Dead Sea Scrolls and Christian Origins* [Grand Rapids, MI: Eerdmans, 2000] 73). Both he, in the article cited above, and J. H. Charlesworth (*The Messiah: Developments in Earliest Judaism and Christianity: The First Princeton Symposium on Judaism and Christian Origins* [Minneapolis, MN: Fortress, 1992]) give a good sense of the problem, namely, the slippery nature of the use of this title. More recently, there is J. Fitzmyer, *The One Who Is To Come*. Grand Rapids, MI: Eerdmans, 2007.

17   http://www.vatican.va/roman_curia/congregations/cfaith/pcb_ documents/rc_con_cfaith_doc_20020212_ popoloebraico_en.html#2.% 20Rereading%20the%20Old%20Testament%20in%20the%20light%20o f%20Christ. §21.

18   The term *kyrios* translates the tetragrammaton only in such LXX manuscripts as were copied by Christian scribes. It has been shown that *kyrios*, *adôn*, and *mare* were all used by pre-Christian Palestinian Jews for Yahweh. (Fitzmyer, "New Testament Kyrios and Maranatha and their Aramaic Background," *TAG*, 220-23).

19   Letter (X.25 ff) from Pliny to the Emperor Trajan (about 112 AD).

20   Chapter 20 was the original conclusion of the gospel. What editors call "the epilogue" (chapter 21) was added later. For more on this see R.E. Brown. *The Gospel of John*. 2 vols. (AB 29, 29A; New York: Doubleday, 1966).

21   Though the Gospel of John mentions Jesus' mother, she is never

named (John 2:1,3,5,12; 6:42; 19:25,26). We need the Synoptic Gospels and Acts to know that her name was Mary (e.g., Acts 1:14).

22 This is the version that Catholics pray since Vatican II (1962-1965). This is a dynamic, or loose, translation of the Latin. However, the particular words that concern us here, Blessed Mary ever Virgin, are a direct translation of *beatam Mariam semper Vírginem*, which is in the pre-Vatican II Latin version of the prayer, and the post-Vatican II version of the prayer.

23 Scholars refer to this as a creedal fragment. By that they mean the verbiage existed prior to Paul. Paul draws from it and employs it here in Rom 1:3-4 because it suits his purpose. This is called a fragment rather than a statement because it begins with a relative pronoun (who). Examples of early creedal statements would be "Jesus is Lord" (Rom 10:9). For more on Rom 1:3-4 see Fitzmyer, *Romans*.

24 Translation from Michael W. Holmes (ed. and rev.) *The Apostolic Fathers: Greek Texts and English Translations*. (Grand Rapids: MI; Baker, 1999) 141.

25 W. R. Schoedel, *Ignatius of Antioch: A Commentary on the Letters of Ignatius of Antioch* (Hermeneia; Philadelphia: Fortress, 1985) 20.

26 cf. Josephus, *Jewish Wars* 2.169-177; *Jewish Antiquities* 18.55-59,62,85-87; Philo. *On the Embassy to Gaius*, 301-302.

27 Fitzmyer, J. *Acts* (AB 31; New York: Doubleday, 1998) 391.

28 Pontifical Biblical Commission, *The Jewish People and their Sacred Scriptures in the Christian Bible*, 2002, §71. Available online at: http://www.vatican.va/roman_curia/congregations/cfaith/pcb_documents/rc_con_cfaith_doc_20020212_popolo-ebraico_en.html.

29 Appian, *Civil Wars*, 1.120.

30 For more on this important issue, see the recent book, J. Fitzmyer. *The One Who Is To Come*. Grand Rapids, MI: Eerdmans, 2007.

31 http://www.vatican.va/roman_curia/congregations/cfaith/pcb_documents/rc_con_cfaith_doc_20020212_ popoloebraico_en.html#2.%20Rereading%20the%20Old%20Testament%20in%20the%20light%20o f%20Christ. §21.

32 Koran 4.157 http://www.irvl.net/koran.pdf.

33 There are many studies on the life and chronology of Paul. A sketch of his life can be found in the article "Paul" §79 in the *NJBC*. A more detailed study can be found in J. Murphy-O'Connor. *Paul: A Critical Life*. Oxford: New York, 1996.

34 http://newsweek.washingtonpost.com/onfaith/susan_jacoby/2007/09/the_theodicy_problem_no_proble.ht ml. Blog posting 9/5/2007.

35 Eph 4:9 speaks of a descent into the lower regions of the earth, but this is not the "*inferna*."

36 Rufinus, *A Commentary on the Apostles' Creed* §18 in ACW 20.52 (trans. J.N.D. Kelly).

37 The term *gehenna* is found in twelve places in the New Testament: Matt 5:22,29,30; 10:28; 18:9; 23:15,33; Mark 9:43,45,47; Luke 12:5; Jas 3:6.

38 D. F. Watson. "Gehenna" ABD. 2.927-8.

39 *et propter hoc Dominum in ea quae sunt sub terra descendisse evangelizantem et illis adventum suum, remissionem peccatorum exsistentem his qui credunt in eum* (AH 4.27.2 in SC 100.738).

40 J. E. Elliott. 1 Peter (AB 37B; New York: Doubleday, 2000) 709, cf. 706-710.

41 Pope John Paul II, General Audience, January 11, 1989. Available online in Italian and Spanish. http://www.vatican.va/holy_father/john_paul_ii/audiences/1989/documents/hf_jp-ii_aud_19890111_it.html

Translation here is my own from the Italian.

La Parola del Vangelo e della Croce tutti raggiunge, anche quelli appartenenti alle generazioni passate più lontane, perché tutti coloro che si sono salvati sono stati resi partecipi della Redenzione, anche prima che avvenisse l'evento storico del sacrificio di Cristo sul Golgota. … Questa è la "verità" che si può trarre dai testi biblici citati e che è espressa nell'articolo del Credo che parla di "discesa agli inferi".

42 *USCCA*, 93.

43 R. E. Brown. *The Death of the Messiah*. 2 vols. (ABRL; New York: Doubleday, 1994) 2.1320.

44 For example, if the earth were rotating on its axis, it would make one complete 24,000 mile rotation in 24 hours. Another way to think of that is to say that everything on the earth is traveling at about 1000 miles/hour. If that is the case, why don't we fall off the earth? How do birds even fly? Why don't clouds simply dissipate or become wispy bands across the sky?

Furthermore, if the earth were rotating on its own axis, it would necessarily be revolving around the sun. The Greeks also estimated the distance of the earth to the sun at millions of miles (though the actual distance is about 93 million miles). Thus, on any given night the stars appear in certain locations. Six months later, when the earth is millions of miles away from where it was six months earlier (186 million miles to be more precise), why don't the stars appear to be in different locations with respect to one another? (Not to mention the speed with which the earth would need to travel to get to that point in six months. Rotation on its axis at 1000 miles per hour and revolution around the sun at speeds even greater than that combined to create an incredibly violent and fantastic image of the earth's movement that was too much to accept). This effect is known as stellar parallax, and was in fact demonstrated fairly recently. The required precision for instruments to measure that miniscule degree of stellar parallax was not available until the 19th century.

Also, if the stars are so far away, how can we see them at all? They would have to be incredibly bright, and unbelievable large to shine so brightly that we would see them at all. So in fact, the ancients had good reasons for assuming the earth was a stationary sphere, and that the stars, moon, and sun moved around it.

45 Paul's concept of judgment is complicated. At times he speaks of God judging outsiders (1 Cor 5:13). At other times he speaks of the saints or holy ones judging the world and the angels (1 Cor 6:2-3). In some sense we are watching the early Christians forge theology. Paul is reconciling traditional Jewish belief with his experience of the Risen Christ.

46 cf. also Gen 1:2.

47 E.g., Judg 3:10; 6:34; 11:29; 13:25; 14:6,19; 15:14; 1 Sam 10:6; 16:13-14; 2 Sam 23:2; 1 Kgs 22:24 = 2 Chr 18:23; Isa 11:2; 63:14; Ezek 11:5; Mic 3:8; 2 Chr 20:14; Isa 61:1.

48 Exod 31:3; 35:31; Num 24:2; 1 Sam 10:10; 11:16; 19:20,23; 2 Chr 15:1; 24:20.

49 Judg 3:10.

50 1 Sam 10:10; 19:23.

51 I am using here only the undisputed letters of Paul (Rom, 1 and 2 Cor, Gal, Phil, Phlm, and 1 Thess) Rom 1:4,9; 2:29; 5:5; 7:6; 8:2,4,5(bis),6,9(ter),10,11(bis),13,14,15(bis), 16(bis),23,26(bis),27; 9:1; 11:8; 12:11; 14:17; 15:13,16,19,30; 1 Cor 2:4,10(bis),11(bis), 12(bis),13,14; 3:16; 4:21; 5:3,4,5; 6:11,17,19; 7:34, 40; 12:3(bis),4,7,8(bis),9(bis),10 ,11, 13(bis); 14:2,12,14,15(bis),16,32; 15:45; 16:18; 2 Cor 1:22; 2:13; 3:3,6(bis),8,17(bis),18; 4:13; 5:5; 6:6; 7:1,13; 11:4; 12:18; 13:13; Gal 3:2,3,5,14; 4:6,29; 5:5,16,17(bis),18,22, 25(bis); 6:1,8(bis),18; Phil

1:19,27; 2:1; 3:3; 4:23; 1 Thess 1:5,6; 4:8; 5:19,23; Phlm 1:25.

52 Rom 2:9; 11:3; 13:1; 16:4; 1 Cor 15:45; 2 Cor 1:23; 12:15; Phil 1:27; 2:30; 1 Thess 2:8; 5:23.

53 Fitzmyer, *Romans*, 127. Paul uses *pneuma* in an anthropological sense to refer to that aspect of the person which is open to receive the Spirit of God, or the means by which a person relates most directly to God: "for God is my witness, whom I serve with my spirit by announcing the gospel of his Son, that without ceasing I remember you always in my prayers" (Rom 1:9). Later in the same letter Paul claims: "it is the Spirit itself bearing witness with our spirit that we are children of God" (Rom 8:16).

54 Scholars do disagree as to whether Paul uses "Lord" in this verse to refer to Christ (Ridderbos Paul, 87) or to "'the Lord' of the text just adapted" (Dunn, Theology, 422). Ridderbos cites 2 Cor 3:17 as an example where "Christ and the Spirit are placed in a certain relationship of identity with each other."

55 Schweizer, "*pneuma, pneumatikos*," *TDNT*, 6.436.

56 The phrase *to pneuma tou anthrōpou to en autō(i)* (the human spirit within) serves as an example of *pneuma* referring to the innermost depths of a person.

57 "yet we speak about wisdom to those who are mature, but not about a wisdom of this age, or even of the rulers of this age who are passing away" (1 Cor 2:6).

58 The phrase to *pneuma mou* is best translated "the Spirit given to me" rather than "my spirit," or "my innermost spiritual being" (Barrett, *First Epistle*, 320; pace A.C Thiselton, *The First Epistle to the Corinthians* [NIGTC; Grand Rapids, MI: Eerdmans, 2000] 1110). Paul is not so much setting up a dichotomy between spirit and mind in an individual, but a dichotomy between the Spirit and the mind as vv. 15-16 indicate. Furthermore, Rom 8:26 echoes this idea: "in the same way, the Spirit also comes to the aid of our weakness; for we do not know what to pray for as we ought, but the Spirit itself intercedes with inutterable groanings."

59 In Gal 5:19b-21a Paul lists examples of the works of the flesh: "illicit sexual union, fornication, uncleanness, licentiousness, idolatry, sorcery, hatred, strife, jealousy, wrath, quarrels, divisions, factions, envy, drunkenness, carousing and the like."

60 Though there is no Old Testament evidence to suggest a rivalry between Ishmael and Isaac, such a rivalry is referred to in later rabbinic sources.

61 F. J. Matera, *Galatians* (SacPag 9; Collegeville, MN: Liturgical, 1992) 216.

62 *Rite of Baptism for Children* §97, 148, et al. in, *The Rites of the Catholic Church*. New York: Pueblo Publishing, 1976.

63 4.171 www.irvl.net/koran.pdf.

64 The noun *hagios* is used 233 times in the New Testament (Concordance to the Novum Testamentum Graece of Nestle-Aland, 26th Edition, and the Greek New Testament, 3rd Edition. [3rd ed. De Gruyter. New York, 1987] 20-26).

65 Lumen Gentium §41 accessed online at http://www.vatican.va/archive/hist_councils/ii_vatican_council/documents/vat-ii_const_19641121_lumen-gentium_en.html.

66 Martin Luther, *Larger Catechism*.

67 Congregation for the Doctrine of the Faith. Responses to some questions regarding certain aspects of the doctrine of the church. June 27, 2007. Available online at: http://www.vatican.va/roman_curia/congregations/cfaith/documents/rc_con_cfaith_doc_20070629_

responsa-quaestiones_en.html.

68 Luke 1:77; 3:3; 24:47; Acts 2:38; 5:31; 10:43; 13:38; 26:18.

69 Meier, John P., A Marginal Jew: Rethinking the Historical Jesus. 2 vol. New York: Doubleday, 1994. 291-302.

70 Meier, A Marginal Jew. 2. 292-293.

71 Cf. CCC §1436.

72 Credimus etiam veram resurrectionem huius carnis, quam nunc gestamus DS §854.

73 E.g. Laura Sheahen ("The Resurrection of the Body." America. Vol. 196 no. 12, April 2, 2007) writes an article questioning, "Why doesn't bodily resurrection interest, much less delight, people who are otherwise devout?"

74 dicentibusque nobis, utrum capillos et dentes, pectus ac uentrem, manus et pedes ceterosque artus ex integro resurrectio exhibeat, tunc uero se tenere non possunt cachinnoque ora soluentes tonsores nobis necessarios et placentas et medicos ac sutores ingerunt ultroque interrogant, utrum credamus et genitalia utriusque sexus resurgere, nostras genas hirtas, feminarum leues fore et habitudinem corporis pro maris ac feminae distinctione diuersam. quod si dederimus, statim expetunt uuluam et coitum et cetera, quae in uentre sunt et sub uentre. singula membra negant et corpus, quod constat ex membris, dicunt resurgere. Epistula 84.5 (CSEL 55. 127).

75 dioper ou kakōs potamon ōnamastai to sōma. PG 12. 1093.

76 As the liturgy of the church states (Roman Missal, Preface of Christian Death I, also quoted in CCC §1012):

Lord, for your faithful people life is changed, not ended.
When the body of our earthly dwelling lies in death
we gain an everlasting dwelling place in heaven.

77 Plato believed in a realm of the forms. That is, there was an immaterial realm where true beauty, true goodness, true unity and other qualities existed. He believed that this material world shares in the realm of the forms, participates in it. So that, each object of beauty in the material world is in some way a reflection of the true form of beauty. Each object of goodness in the material world is a reflection of the true form of goodness. Plato further held that our immortal souls existed in this realm of the forms before we were born. Thus, after we die our immortal souls will return to this realm of the forms.

78 Quemadmodum enim qui est a terra panis, percipiens invocationem Dei, jam non communis panis est, sed Eucharistia, ex duabus rebus constans, terrena et caelesti: sic et corpora nostra percipientia Eucharistiam jam non sunt corruptibilia, spem resurrectionis habentia (AH 4.18.5. [SC 100. 610,612]; cf. 5.2.3).

79 Credimus etiam veram resurrectionem huius carnis, quam nunc gestamus, et vitam aeternam DS§854.

80 Taken from http://www.vatican.va/archive/hist_councils/ii_vatican_council/documents/vat-ii_cons_19651207_gaudium-et-spes_en.html.

81 Paragraphs §1061-1065 in the Catechism have to do with the final word of the creed, Amen.

Appendices

A-1. General Timeline

Year	Event/person
27/30	Death of Jesus
20 B.C. – A.D. 50	Philo of Alexandria
64/67	Death of Peter and Paul
ca. 95	*1 Clement*
ca. 37-100	Josephus
ca. 117	Death of Ignatius of Antioch
ca. 69-155	Polycarp
ca. 63-113	Pliny (the Younger)
r. 98-117	Trajan (Roman Emperor)
ca. 100-165	Justin Martyr
ca. 110-160	Marcion
fl. 176-180	Athenagoras
ca. 125-200	Irenaeus of Lyons
ca. 150-216	Clement of Alexandria
ca. 150-230	Tertullian
ca. 185-254	Origen
d. ca. 240	Hippolytus of Rome
325	Council of Nicea
ca. 320-403	Epiphanius of Salamis
345-410	Rufinus
347-420	Jerome
354-430	Augustine
1225-1274	Thomas Aquinas
1274	Second General Council of Lyons
1483-1546	Martin Luther
1545-1563	Council of Trent
1566	Roman Catechism
1962-1965	Vatican II
1964-1978	Pontificate of Paul VI
1978-2004	Pontificate of John Paul II
1992	*Catechism of the Catholic Church*, 1st edition
1997	*Catechism of the Catholic Church*, 2nd edition
2004	Pontificate of Benedict XVI
2006	*United States Catholic Catechism for Adults*

A-2.   Apostles' Creed

I BELIEVE IN GOD *the Father almighty creator of heaven and earth.*

I believe in Jesus Christ, his only Son, our Lord.

He was conceived by the power of the Holy Spirit and born of the Virgin Mary.

He suffered under Pontius Pilate, was crucified, died, and was buried.

He descended into hell. On the third day he rose again.

He ascended into heaven and is seated at the right hand of the Father.

He will come again to judge the living and the dead.

I believe in the Holy Spirit, the holy catholic Church, the communion of saints, the forgiveness of sins, the resurrection of the body, and the life everlasting.

Amen.

A-3.   Nicene Creed

WE BELIEVE IN ONE GOD, *the Father, the Almighty, maker of heaven and earth, of all that is seen and unseen.*

We believe in one Lord, Jesus Christ, the only Son of God eternally begotten of the Father, God from God, Light from Light, true God from true God, begotten not made, one in being with the Father. Through him all things were made. For us men and our salvation he came down from heaven:

by the power of the Holy Spirit he was born of the Virgin Mary, and became man

For our sake he was crucified under Pontius Pilate; he suffered, died, and was buried.

On the third day he rose again in fulfillment of the Scriptures;

he ascended into heaven and is seated at the right hand of the Father. He will come again in glory to judge the living and the dead and his kingdom will have no end.

We believe in the Holy Spirit, the Lord, the giver of life, who proceeds from the Father and the Son. With the Father and the Son he is worshipped and glorified. He has spoken through the prophets.

We believe in one holy catholic and apostolic Church.

We acknowledge one baptism for the forgiveness of sins.

We look for the resurrection of the dead, and the life of the world to come. Amen.

A-4.   Lists of the Twelve*

Mark 3:16-19	Matthew 10:2-4	Luke 6:14-16	Acts 1:13
First Group of Four			
Simon Peter	Simon Peter	Simon Peter	Peter
James (son of) Zebedee	Andrew his brother	Andrew his brother	John
John brother of James	James (son of) Zebedee	James	James
Andrew	John his brother	John	Andrew
Second Group of Four			
Philip	Philip	Philip	Philip
Bartholomew	Bartholomew	Bartholomew	Thomas
Matthew	Thomas	Matthew	Bartholomew
Thomas	Matthew the toll Collector	Thomas	Matthew
Third Group of Four			
James (son of) Alphaeus	James (son of) Alphaeus	James (son of) Alphaeus	James (son of) Alphaeus
Thaddeus	Thaddeus	Simon the Zeaolot	Simon the Zealot
Simon the Cananean	Simon the Cananean	Jude (of) James	Jude (of) James
Judas Iscariot	Judas Iscariot	Judas Iscariot	———

* Many scholars have examined the lists of the twelve. I find particularly helpful the arrangement of John Meier (*A Marginal Jew*. vol. 3. [New York: Doubleday, 2001] 130), on which this page is based.

DR. BRIAN SCHMISEK

Dr. Brian Schmisek is the Dean of the School of Ministry
at the University of Dallas. He holds a Ph.D. in Biblical
Studies from The Catholic University of America, and Masters
degrees in Classics from the University of Mississippi and
Theology from The Catholic University of America. In his five
years at the University of Dallas, Brian has overseen the
growth of the School to its current enrollment of over 900
students. Brian believes strongly in bringing the resources
of the academy to serve the church and larger world. This
belief is reflected in the various programs offered now by the
School of Ministry including graduate degree programs in
ministry that include a Masters in Catholic School Teaching,
a Catholic Biblical School offered in English and in Spanish,
face to face, and online, Adult Faith Formation programs,
deacon formation, and much more. His interests are clearly
in making theology meaningful and applicable. Brian and his
wife, Marnie have four children.